The Uncommon
Written For Pa:
To Help Your Teen Become Extraordinary

By

Cayden Tomlin, Jackson Tomlin, and Zach Stoner

Contents

Acknowledgments 3

Endorsements 5

Bios 6

Foreword 8

Introduction 9

    1. Excellence As A Teen 13

    2. To Date or Not to Date 22

    3. Friends 30

    4. Your Outgoing Teen 34

    5. The Gift of Encouragement 39

    6. How to Destroy the Root of All Sin 44

    7. Good Dad, Great Dad 51

    8. Walking From Death to Life 59

    9. T.G.I.M Teen 65

    10. Teenwork: How to Inspire Your Teen to Love Working 70

    11. Your Child's Obsession with Electronics 78

    12. Money 85

    13. Works Cited 93

FAQ's 95

ACKNOWLEDGMENTS

Thanks to Student Leadership University for giving us the opportunity to experience world-class leaders, sessions, and lessons. Thanks to Dr. Jay Strack and the entire SLU team. You guys have impacted our lives so much more than we will ever know. Thanks for all you do to impact youth around the world.

Special thanks to SLU Vice President Dr. Brent Crowe for his support and feedback of the book, and for accepting the opportunity to endorse it in the first place. Thanks for taking the time to hear two teenage guys in the streets of Oxford make the most awkward book pitch of all time, and then jumping on board.

Thanks to the following photographers: Roland Heddins, Neda Morrow, the Lindale HS Digital Editing Class.

We would also like to thank our siblings: Sierra, Savannah, Reagan, Eli, Silas, and Nora. Thanks for bringing so much light into our lives. We love y'all.

Thanks to Riley, Asher, and Jax, for no reason at all, aside from the fact that you are the cutest dogs on Planet Earth. Don't ever change.

Thanks to our moms, Brandy and Alisa, who dutifully spent hours reading and editing our chapters. You're the best. We will proudly carry on the homeschool legacy.

Also, thanks to our grandparents: Cayden and Jackson's Grandpa/Grandma (Craig and Gwen) and Deedee/Papa (Donna and Connie), and Zach's Grandpa/Grandma (Bill and Marilyn) and Mimi/Pop Pop (Wendy and Chris). You guys have poured into us for years. We love y'all.

Also, thanks to Kevin and Stephanie Cool for looking over, editing and giving feedback to our book. That, and the laughter you bring to any conversation is much appreciated. Hope to see you at the Old West Café soon.

Thank you, Penny Snow, Annie Cochran, Carol Hammons and Patti Spann for taking the time out of your busy schedule to critique and edit our book. We don't always use the best grammar, so we is thankin' you for teachin' us peeps to using that grammar. You is muchly appreciated. (We should have asked you to proof-read this).

Thanks to Chris Tomlin, for finding time to write a foreword while juggling a million things at once. That's what true family does. Never Lose Sight.

And finally, special thanks to Ryan and Heath. Thanks for pushing us and for inspiring us to write this book. None of this is possible without your ideas, vision, and your determination to see your boys succeed. You both are the perfect example of the Great Dad. Love you.

ENDORSEMENTS

I have been incredibly privileged to watch Cayden, Jackson, and Zach grow into exemplary young men of God. I remember walking the streets at Oxford University listening to them share the incredible vision that would become *The Uncommon Teenager*. And now that it is completed I can say with confidence, *IT IS AMAZING!!!* For any parent wanting a backstage pass to the inner longings of your child's heart, this book is written for you! And for any teenager wanting to rise above average while treading water in a sea of cultural mediocrity; this resource is a lighthouse that can guide you a life of God-honoring excellence.

Brent Crowe, PH.D Vice President, Student Leadership University

Zach, Cayden and Jackson have written a great book for teens and parents. This book is full of real-life stories from teenage guys who are living what they are writing about. Their advice to other teens and to parents is solid, usable, and refreshing. I was challenged in my own parenting philosophies and encouraged that I am doing a lot of things right. I highly recommend this book for parents who are looking for insights into teenagers' minds and want to improve their parenting skills. I highly recommend it for parents of teens who genuinely want to become extraordinary and are willing to apply effort toward that end.

David Hasz (Father, Husband, EVP/Provost of Bethany Global University)

BIOS

Meet Cayden

My name is Cayden Tomlin; I was born November 18, 2003. I currently reside in Mineola, Texas, but I grew up in Bullard, Texas. I have five siblings that are 2, 3, 5, 10, and 13. Three of them were adopted, but will share that later in the book. I have been homeschooled since 2nd grade, and I go to a small Co-op in Lindale, Texas. Some things I like to do are play basketball, hang out with friends, and watch movies. I play basketball for a home school team in Tyler, Texas, called Heat. I was inspired to write this book because my dad has taught me to be different, and there are not many teens writing books on real-life topics. I get to portray what I believe as a Christian to parents and teens and hit on topics like excellence, friends, electronics, and the gift of encouraging others. I feel like this book will open so many parents and teens eyes to today's most pressing issues and will have a massive impact on our generation. Come and enjoy the journey with me!

Meet Jackson

My name is Jackson Tomlin and I was born December 2, 2005. I have grown up in East Texas my whole life. My family consists of my mom and dad, my brothers Cayden, Elijah and Silas, and my sisters Reagan and Nora. My favorite things to do are play sports (mainly basketball) and hanging out with friends. I also like to go to the beach in the summer, and snow ski in the winter. I enjoy going to our family lake house where we water ski and have quality family time. Every Monday I go to a homeschool co-op called Classical Conversations. The co-op lays out our work for the week and sets the tone for what needs to be accomplished to share in class the following Monday. In the summer, I go to a leadership camp called Student Leadership University where we learn how to be leaders and influencers for our generation. The main reason that I wanted to write this book is to inspire and motivate my generation to live with purpose. As time goes on, the world is coming out with new things to draw us away from the main purpose for which we were created: to glorify God and make him known. I hope to encourage parents to be involved in their teens life and pray constantly with them as they go through highs and lows.

Meet Zach

My name is Zach Stoner. I was born in 2002 in East Texas, and have lived there my whole life. I have an awesome set of parents, Heath and Alisa; two awesome younger sisters, Sierra and Savannah; and two awesome dogs, Asher and Jax. My dad is a youth pastor and an administrator at Tyler Junior College. My mom is tasked with the infinitely harder job of homeschooling us three kids. I most enjoy quality time spent with God, family, and friends. I enjoy sports (especially basketball) as well as reading, video games, movies, and driving. Like around 95% of teenage guys, I enjoy food, especially Takis, Chipotle, pizza, and ice cream. Other interests include marine biology, puns, school, and traveling. My favorite vacation spot is Europe, where I attended a youth leadership conference called Student Leadership University. For the third phase of the four-year program, we went to London, Paris, Oxford, and Normandy.

Student Leadership University helped inspire me to write this book. Throughout this book the Tomlins and I have written and incorporated many ideas we learned at SLU into our chapters, and some have even become entire chapter topics (Excellence). Another reason I was challenged to write this book was the values that my family has instilled in me, and realizing how few teens today are set up for a full and abundant life in adulthood. It could be family issues, an attitude of rebellion towards authority, or the most likely option, teens today have become so influenced and bombarded by the culture and have become slaves to popularity, media, and so many other vices. When I realized that I could make a difference, I jumped at the chance to write this book. I hope you and your teen are encouraged and are better prepared for equipping your teen for the future.

FOREWORD

Yes, it is true. Teenagers can be know-it-alls. For many, it is at this age, when most refuse to listen to their parents' wisdom and advice. This book, however, turns this entire notion upside down. Yes, it is written from teenagers to parents, but maybe not in a way you would expect. It is a call for parents to step up and lead them, to teach and train them in the most important areas and aspects of life. What a unique approach and voice for a book! It flies in the face of our current youth culture in so many ways. The Uncommon Teenager is filled with solid, practical Life 101 skills, but much deeper than this, is a heart to honor and glorify God.

I hope you are as encouraged as I am to know there are young men and women in the coming generations who desire to walk with God in such a real and true way. I am proud of these three young men for bringing the vision of this book to life. Two of them just happen to be my nephews!

Chris Tomlin

INTRODUCTION

Before we get into the meat of this book, you need a basic understanding of Gen Z. Our generation. What makes us tick? What are we about? What do we believe?

Gen Z are the ones born between 1999 and 2015. According to a Biola and Talbot alumni study on Gen Z, "They're vastly different from their millennial predecessors—less religious, more success-oriented, more diverse, more captivated by technology, and more likely to embrace different views on sexual identity."

One of the alumni who headed the study calls Gen Z "screenagers", and he's not wrong. "'More than half of teens use screen media four or more hours per day,' the alumnus said. 'That's about 57 percent. About 26 percent use screen media eight or more hours per day. They are also the first generation to be raised by parents who are on screens, and that's one of the things that makes them different than millennials.'"

A 2018 study by Barna Research Group shows that almost a quarter of Gen Z "strongly agrees that what is morally right and wrong changes over time based on society." One participant in the study was quoted: "Society changes, and what's good or bad changes as well. It is all relative to what's happening in the world."

Throughout the entire Barna study, research indicates incredible generational gaps between our generation and others such as Baby Boomers and Elders. For instance, one-third of Gen Z believes lying is wrong. In the oldest generation—Elders—three in five strongly agree that lying is morally wrong. Disapproval of homosexuality also increases when you rise by generation.

The Barna study showed encouraging statistics for Engaged Christian Gen Z compared to lukewarm Christians. But first; what are 'Engaged Christians'? The study defined them as ones identifying as a Christian, having attended church in the past six months, and strongly agreeing with the ultimate truth of the Bible, having made a personal and impactful decision for Jesus Christ, engaging with church in numerous ways, and believing that Jesus was crucified and then raised from the dead to conquer our sin and death. Lukewarm Christians, or 'Churched Christians' identified as Christians and attended church within half a year, but did not qualify for the above definitions.

Now to the stats. Engaged Christians are 77% likely to say that lying is immoral, while churched Christians are only 38% likely to agree. More than three-quarters of Engaged Christians believe sex before marriage and homosexuality are wrong, while only one-quarter of Churched Christians believed sex out of wedlock and homosexuality were wrong. Keep in mind that these statistics apply *only* to those in Gen Z.

But what's the overall belief? What's the vibe? According to the Barna study, "Gen Z as a whole are generally opposed to challenging others' beliefs, likely driven by a desire to avoid offense or to acknowledge the value of other perspectives." However, when talking about the Engaged Christians, "Engaged Christian teens (and adults, for that matter) are twice as likely as their peers to strongly disagree that 'if your beliefs offend someone or hurt their feelings, they are probably wrong.' That is, two-thirds do not equate the truth of their beliefs with how appealing (or unappealing) they are to others."

In conclusion, our generation listens. We listen to our parents , but we don't always obey. We listen to our elders, to our authorities, to our peers, again, not always obeying. We hear all these points of view. We see how, in today's culture, you can be condemned as a hater for disagreeing with an opposing point of view. And so, afraid of being attacked, we stay silent. We may or may not agree, but we are afraid to offend people. We acknowledge others' opinions. We just don't always voice *our own* opinions to others. On social media, you can say anything you want, and you will get pushback. But at the teenage level, you're not risking anything. You aren't risking a job, or a career, or an opportunity. But when you are face-to-face with someone? That's a whole other story. Don't offend them. Be loving. Agree with everyone. So, says America.

We lack conviction. We lack the voice that many other groups have. People stereotype us and say we are too caught up in technology. We are. But that's not the only reason. We are afraid of being called a hater, or a bigot, or racist, or sexist, or whatever. Instead of pushing back, we cower behind. Sometimes that's not a bad thing. But when an entire generation stays silent, what voices are they going to share when they are the ones in authority?

Those who are strong Christians, who deeply love and long to know Christ, we know more or less what we believe. We know when someone is wrong. We disagree, but not in a hating, condemning way (usually). But what about those of us who don't know what they believe? They shut up. Because the culture is telling them to shut up, *unless* you agree with what *they* believe.

Be loving, yes. God calls us to love one another. I fully believe that. Without love, I am naught but a clanging cymbal. Without love, I am nothing (I Cor. 13).

But in today's society, *loving* has become synonymous with *agreeing*. If you disagree with someone, how could you possibly love them? Our culture questions. If you voted for someone other than who I voted for, you can't love me because you don't agree with me, and I am *always* right!

Is it just me, or is there a problem going on here?

What you are about to read is tailored to help your teen's generation find a voice. To instill in them the confidence of their beliefs and to protect them from falling into the snares of the enemy. To help them with struggles that every teen face, and to bring them out battle-tested and ready to face the next season of their life. Our generation has become sluggish and quiet. It is time for Gen Z to rise. To strive for excellence. To become Uncommon.

Are you ready to help them?

Excellence As A Teen

A German once visited a temple under construction where he saw a sculptor making an idol of god.

Suddenly, he noticed a similar idol lying nearby.

Surprised, he asked the sculptor, "Do you need two statues of the same idol?"

"No," said the sculptor without looking up, "We need only one, but the first one got damaged at the last stage."

The gentleman examined the idol and found no apparent damage.

"Where is the damage?" he asked.

"There is a scratch on the nose of the idol." said the sculptor, still busy with his work.

"Where are you going to install the idol?"

The sculptor replied that it would be installed on a pillar twenty feet high.

"If the idol is that far, who is going to know that there is a scratch on the nose?" the gentleman asked.

The sculptor stopped work, looked up at the gentleman, smiled and said, "I will know it."

Excellent in Your Work

Have you ever compared your teen to the characteristic of an animal? If so, what animal would you compare your teen to? We can all agree that a sloth would not be a positive comparison. Most of us can relate to being lazy and sluggish at some point in our lives, but this is a very costly habit to form. Idleness can play a major part in your teen's lazy habits, but like the story above, excellence needs to play apart in how we operate. My dad has always told my brother and I to be excellent in our work, whether it be in labor, school work, or hobbies. Parents, pay attention to details in your teen's life, calling out work that is unfinished, sloppy, or set aside for another time. My work has improved by the constant reminder from my parents about the quality, not quantity of work I perform. Laborious work, such as mowing, weed eating, unloading dishes, cleaning, laundry, or other chores need to be a part of your teens day to teach excellence in work. When you (the parent) are excellent, teaching your teen excellence, you are setting an example that your teen will model as they transition into adulthood. Being the oldest of five, constantly being taught excellence, has prompted me to be an example to them, and most importantly, act like Jesus. My family adopted three children, and they have not had good exposure to what a nurturing, loving and disciplined home looks like, so it is imperative I set the tone for them as you would want an older teen setting the tone for the younger siblings. It is our job to set a good example, showing them what a good work ethic is, and this is not just to my brother and sister, but to any kids we are around. I hope to encourage you to keep excellence as your focus in all areas of your teen's life. Colossians 3:17 says," And whatever you do, whether in word or deed, do it all in the name of the Lord Jesus, giving thanks to God the Father through him." Excellence breeds confidence, and confidence leads to a teen influencing the circles of people they are around, and impacting our generation to promote excellence in every word and deed.

"All I ever wanted really, and continue to want out of life, is to give one-hundred percent to whatever I'm doing and to be committed, and then let the results speak for themselves. Also, never take myself or people for granted and always be thankful and grateful to the people who helped me."- Jackie Joyner-Kersee

Doing Things Halfway

School is hard, especially between schedule demands and activities. Throughout the year, parents must be intentional with their teen, making sure they're not slacking in the area of excellence. We try to live out what Colossians 3:23 says, "Whatever you do, work heartily, as for the Lord and not for men." Being too busy is a major area of concern and roadblock to excellence. Parents have to be intentional, making sure their teen is not doing things halfway. My family has chosen to homeschool, so I don't have a school district counting on me to perform at state standards. However, with the pushing of my parents, I have chosen to be better in the areas of internal motivation.

How would you rate your teen right now in the area of internal or external motivation? Are they more apt to be excellent with your external motivation or developed internal motivation? External motivation only works for a while; and usually, all involved are exhausted from it, but internal motivation is long lasting and is what drives teenagers to become excellent at an early age. My dad always asked us, "Whatever you are doing, are you an asset or a liability?" My question for you in the area of excellence: are your teens an asset or a liability in your home?Martin Luther King, Jr. petitioned, "If a man is called to be a street sweeper, he should sweep streets even as Michelangelo painted, or Beethoven composed music, or Shakespeare wrote poetry. He should sweep streets so well that all the hosts of heaven and earth will pause to say, 'Here lived a great street sweeper who did his job well'."

Confidence

"For the LORD will be your confidence and will keep your foot from being caught" (Proverbs 3:26). This proverb is profound in establishing the foundation of confidence and God is who we need to place it in. We need to place our confidence in Christ which gives correct perspective of confidence and excellence in ourselves.

Excellence promotes a greater confidence in teenagers, as well as establishing a greater confidence in their education, sporting events, hobbies, and interpersonal skills.

How do you react when your teen is faced with adversity? Hopefully, during these formative years, you are embracing adversity with your teen instead of enduring it. We all fail and lose confidence through life events and circumstances we cannot control, so instilling excellence allows your teen to overcome difficulties.

I know teens my age that are insecure, socially awkward, and have begun a road of depression. Creating an environment where excellence is priority, empowers them to face life's many obstacles confidently. In my short fifteen years on earth, I see a connection between procrastination, sloppiness, and laziness that leads down a path of poor choices due to insecurity and lack of confidence. A very important skill my dad has instilled in us is approaching adults with eye contact and a handshake while introducing yourself. I remember starting this long before my teenage years. As he would tell us, "Be excellent in how you introduce yourself. Your first impression is very important." This has led to a confidence that has set me apart from other teens, and I will carry this with me from now on. It is not too late to teach this skill.

 A few more tools that have been instilled in me that show a life of confidence from excellence are choosing of friends that increase my confidence, and talks at night with my dad about issues that challenge us. I highly suggest you start this if you have not. Assign hard things that challenge your teen such as, reading books, writing a book, a part time job, or adventure races. Challenges will produce a more confident teen.

 I am not totally clear what has changed over all the years, but I do know teens stuck in adolescent age seems to be increasing. In an article from the Journal of Psychiatry Neuroscience, JPN states:, "The expanded definition of adolescence is, however, consistent with both a biological and sociological phenomenon known as the prolongation of adolescence. This refers to earlier pubertal onset, particularly in girls. Similarly, in terms of the social/personal responsibility associated with adult roles, adolescence has extended into the early 20s, with more individuals delaying traditional adult responsibilities (e.g., starting a family or full-time employment, buying property) in contemporary societies". In an article from *Growing Leaders,* Dr. Jean Twenge said in her article, "The whole developmental pathway has slowed way down. Today's 18-year old is acting more like a 15-year old and today's young adults in their 20s is acting more like a teen. This is not so good news." Finally, in the Christian Science Monitor, Stephanie Hanes mentions in her article, "Becoming an adult: why more adolescents now say 'Don't rush me." Many researchers, educators, and parents view this apparent slowdown with concern. They see a generation of young people growing up cocooned, controlled, and ill-prepared for life. College administrators say increasing numbers of students seem unable to function without their parents.

Employers wonder what's wrong with their young workers. Parents look up and realize their 20-year-old doesn't know how to do the laundry, and seems uninterested in driving anywhere. Prolonged adolescence is harming this generation and these articles back that belief.

No matter how old you are now, you are never too young, or too old for success, or going after what you want. Here's a short list of people who accomplished great things at different ages:

1) Helen Keller, at the age of 19 months, became deaf and blind, but that didn't stop her. She was the first deaf and blind person to earn a Bachelor of Arts degree.

2) Mozart was already competent on keyboard and violin; he composed from the age of 5

3) Shirley Temple was 6 when she became a movie star on *Bright Eyes.*

4) Anne Frank was 12 when she wrote *The Diary of Anne Frank*.

5) Ma-gnus Carlson became a chess Grandmaster at the age of 13.

6) Nadia Comaneci was a gymnast from Romania that scored seven perfect 10.0 and won three gold medals at the Olympics at age 14.

7) Tenzin Gyatso was formally recognized as the 14th Dalai Lama in November 1950, at the age of 15.

8) Pele, a soccer superstar, was 17 years old when he won the world cup in 1958 with Brazil.

9) Elvis was a superstar by age 19.

10) John Lennon was 20, and Paul McCartney 18 when the Beatles had their first concert in 1961.

11) Jesse Owens was 22 when he won 4 gold medals in Berlin in 1936.

12) Beethoven was a piano virtuoso by age 23.

What is stopping your teen and me from joining this list?

I believe Roy Bennett says it the best, "One of the best ways to influence people is to make them feel important. Most people enjoy those rare moments when others make them feel important. It is one of the deepest human desires."

Confidence leads to making others feel like they are important. Is there any greater feeling than witnessing your teen make someone feel important? You are the one, parent/guardian who sparks the fire and ignites the firestorm that creates an urge of generosity, kindness, and confidence which carries on for generations. I pray for you, the ones whose fingers are turning these pages, that you will start now praying with your spouse and sons/daughters to begin the journey of excellence.

"It's the action, not the fruit of the action, that's important. You have to do the right thing. It may not be in your power, may not be in your time, that they'll be any fruit. But that doesn't mean you stop doing the right thing. You may never know what results come from your actions. But if you do nothing, there will be no result."

— Mahatma Gandhi

Practical Application

Seven Ways You Can Be Excellent:

1. What Are You Good at And Like To Do?

You need not be great at everything you do. We all have our weaknesses and strengths. Play up your strengths first as these are easy to work with, and it will allow you to gain the confidence you need to build upon other areas. Pick what you are already good at and like to do. Passion fuels your motivation to seek excellence.

2. Practice, Practice, Practice

When you know what you are good at, you need to practice it repeatedly. The experts call this "deliberate practice," which means you know what you need to work on and do it repeatedly. Practice allows you to hone your skills and expertise, and this helps you to be excellent. 3. Secure An Experts Help

You cannot expect to learn everything on your own. Just practice itself will only get you so far. In addition, get someone who is already an expert in your area to coach you. This person should be regarded by his peers as being an expert. A coach is able to show you where you have gone wrong, and this feeds back into your deliberate practice cycle.

4. Expect the Best From Yourself

So, knowing the above is not enough if you do not expect the best from yourself. You must remember that being excellent is about doing. Lip service does not lead to becoming great, so begin practicing and seeking help. Desire and willingness to "do something" is key. Once you decide to be excellent at what you do, expect the best from yourself. Do not just talk about it. Do it!

5. Don't Push Too Hard

There is a tendency for people who strive for excellence. To be excellent at what you do is not being perfect, although that can be a good incentive. It is about being the best that you can offer. So, do your best, and know how to take breaks. You need to rejuvenate and restore. Allow yourself to rest, so you can come back stronger the next day.

6. Joyful Effort

You cannot force yourself to do things just because you want to be excellent at what you do. Your effort must sparked by enthusiasm, which means you are willing to put in the work. Forcing yourself to do certain tasks will not help if your heart's not in it. Of course, there will be cases when you are lazy and force yourself to just get it done. When you have passion, it will make the effort enjoyable as you know the fruits of your pursuit is just a matter of time.

7. Patience

Being excellent at what you do takes time. Hence, you must allow time to take its course. These are the hours you need to clock in order to get the practice. These are what some people refer to as rites of passage. It has to be earned. You cannot expect to be excellent at your work in a hurry.

Now, in this next chapter Zach will talk about dating and how it can be a healthy relationship or not.

To Date or Not to Date

WARNING!!!

The content you are about to read is not approved by Hollywood, bigname rappers, Kardashians, Snapchat, breakup songs, or the producers of *The Bachelor*.

This content is rated F (I'll explain later in the chapter).

This very well may be the most counter-cultural, controversial literary work since pamphlets supporting 2016 presidential nominee Donald J. Trump. You will not hear these ideas at your job, on television, on the news, and most likely not from your friends. You may never even hear this in your church.

That being said, I ask that you would read this chapter with an open mind. If you do not agree with a word I write in this chapter, I hope that you will at least read my point of view, even though it is the opposite of what the entire culture has, is, and will portray. If you still disagree with what I write after you have read the chapter, at least you read it and understand the opposing point of view. I am not condemning specific people, I'm simply bringing into question a certain idea that could prove extremely detrimental to your teen's welfare.

We have written this book to teach both you and your son/daughter tips on how to become wiser. Your teen's wisdom is the key to unlocking a more fulfilled, abundant, satisfying life. If your teen is drawing their wisdom from the Supreme Source, God, and Godly counsel from others, then they should have minimal problems with deciding what is ultimately best for them in life.

With that in mind, let me ask you a question: Is participating in an exclusive relationship with a boyfriend/girlfriend healthy and wise for your teen? Does it ultimately benefit them in any way? Is it God's purpose and design for your teen to start a dating relationship in the early years of junior high or high school?

As a parent, it is your responsibility to help guard your teen from temptations and stumbling blocks. Starting a dating relationship in their early teen years will not help fight those temptations; it will only amplify them. Rarely ever will a teen, especially in today's culture, leave a dating relationship unscathed from some kind of carnal impulse or desire.

What are the possible benefits of a teenager dating in high school? Most people would probably say the following:

1) Practice. Dating in high school is practice for dating later in life when you want to get married. If you don't practice dating before college and beyond, you won't know how to date, and it will be extremely hard to find a potential partner.

From personal experience, I can say that almost every single high school dating relationship I've seen or heard of has not ended well. Dating in high school usually leads to hurt, pain, and emotional trauma, and the relationship eventually ends. For me personally, one of the reasons I don't want to date in high school is the fact that I don't want to cause this level of hurt in another girl. I want to practice dating in the season of my life when I believe I am ready. Why practice in high school when I'm not even ready to lead myself, when I can date later in college, and I'm actually ready to lead myself *and* a girl?

2) It's normal. Boys and girls become romantically attracted to one another starting in the early teens, so why not exercise that attraction and date?

Yes, guys and girls develop interest in each other in the early teens. That is normal. But, is dating during your teens normal? A pew research poll (2015) says that 64% of teens ages 13-17 have never been in a dating relationship.

Think about that! Almost two-thirds of high school students have never dated anyone! Dating today isn't normal; in fact, less people are dating in high school then 20 years ago. So, if you want your teen to be doing something "normal," don't have them date!

Here's another statistic: A 2017 CDC poll says that 40% of high school students have had sex. Now, of course, a percentage of those 40% are kids who just hop from girl to girl, or from guy to guy. They're not really dating; they're just "having fun" and "making the most of the moment," but the majority of that 40% are teens who have been dating. So, concluding from this statistic, if your teen begins dating, there is a two in five chance that they will have sex during their high school years.

If you asked a twelve-year-old if a nine-year-old should start dating, what would they say? Most likely, no. (Unless, of course, they want to be funny and start an interesting conversation.) If you asked a fifteenyear-old if a twelve-year-old should start dating, they would say no. If you asked an eighteen-year old if a fifteen-year-old should start dating, they would share, "No! You're a freshman! Focus on getting through high school first because it's hard, *and* more important!" And finally, if you asked a 22-year-old if an eighteen-year-old should start dating, most would say, "You're about to graduate! You'll have to decide what career to pursue, or what college to attend. You have way too much on your plate for a boyfriend/girlfriend. Wait!"

If your teen looks back in three years, what reaction do you think they'll have to their current dating choices? Will they reminisce over the minutes spent with their "significant other?" Will they recall the awkward moments when they're cuddling together in the presence of their circle of friends? Of course not! All they will remember is the embarrassment, the shame, and the eventual heartbreak when the relationship grows stale.

Now there may be some of you parents who met your spouse in high school. If you are still together and going strong in your marriage, awesome! However, the statistics in this day and age aren't very favorable for high school sweethearts. People today are getting married later than ever before. A 2014 study done by melmagazine.com shows that *less than 2%* of all marriages were between high school sweethearts. To quote the study, "More 18 to 34-year-olds met their current significant other through mutual friends than any other means, including dating apps, at social settings and through work—and most certainly high school." That same study showed that high school sweethearts that do not wait until twenty-five to get married have a higher divorce rate than the average American (fifty-four to thirty-two percent). This means your teen's boyfriend/girlfriend will almost certainly not become your teen's future spouse. There are, of course, exceptions, but 2% odds aren't very favorable.

Yes, your teen will eventually have to cut off their relationship with their current boyfriend/girlfriend. Once that happens, it may never be the same between them. It's incredibly hard to break up with someone and stay "just friends." Either the relationship will completely crumble, leaving even more unnecessary burdens and hurt, or the relationship will simply reboot, leaving your teen in an even worse situation than before. Dating is like going to the mall without any money: You leave either feeling frustrated, or you leave taking something that isn't yours.

If you think about it, by darting to and fro between boyfriends and girlfriends, breaking up with them at a moment's notice, your teen is unknowingly practicing divorce. This may sound a bit harsh, but hear me out. The more and more your teen does it, the easier and easier it will get. When the time comes for them to remain faithful to their spouse, they might just revive those old habits they practiced in their high school years and simply want out. Of course, it's not the same for everybody, but that's just one of the possible consequences that could befall your teen.

There is a difference between dating and courting. Courting would be trying to win someone for a husband or a wife. We call it "dating," but it's not nearly the same as what "dating" is considered to be in high school. By dating in high school, your teen might develop unhealthy tendencies that would translate to the time when they are actively searching for a future spouse. If a teen is involved in a promiscuous, unhealthy, or inappropriate relationship while in high school, those habits will likely resurface when they start looking for a future spouse.

Now, you know the problems and the consequences your teen will have to face if they become involved in a premature relationship. It's your responsibility to act. Sorry, but your teen won't suddenly come to their senses, break down in tears, and apologize for their impulsiveness. Odds are, he or she won't want to stop. You as the parent are going to have to be bold and authoritative when dealing with this problem.

Maybe you didn't know that dating in high school was that bad. In fact, you might have dated as a teenager. However, at your age back then, were you ready for that relationship? Even if you were then, things are much different now.

First off, as noted earlier, your teen will almost certainly never marry their boyfriend/girlfriend. Most importantly, the temptations of lust, sex, and other worldly distractions have become magnified tenfold today with social media and technology. If you don't believe that, reread the statistics at the beginning of the chapter. With celebrities, friends, teachers, the entire culture bombarding students today to feel good, to have fun, to mess around, it is nearly impossible for teens today to not be influenced and not act on it. Trust me, if you had problems and temptations dating in high school, they didn't get fixed in today's high school; they got worse.

Instead of focusing on an exclusive dating relationship, your teen should be focusing on the many friendships they have around them. I told you at the beginning of the chapter this chapter was rated F. The F rating is for Friends. I know this chapter may feel like I've been throwing dating into the dirt, rubbing it around, and then chucking it in the trash. In some cases, dating in high school is okay. I've known several people who kept themselves pure while dating in high school. However, they were, for the most part, dedicated Christians and put God first before others. Most teens today, however, do not have that self-discipline. So instead, I would like to propose an alternative to dating: friendships. While it would usually be unhealthy for your son to be involved in a dating relationship with another girl or vice versa, becoming just friends with other girls/guys can be extremely healthy. When you become good friends with a girl (speaking to the guys), you realize that they don't exist just to satisfy your momentary pleasures. I've heard the expression, "Don't do anything to a woman that you wouldn't want someone doing to your sister or your mother." Having innocent friendships with other girls can help strengthen that belief.

My parents have greatly impressed upon me the importance of keeping myself clean and pure going into marriage. Never, at any point in my life, have I believed that dating before high school is acceptable for me. Even now, I understand that I don't need a girlfriend; and besides, I don't even have time for one! With school, sports, work, family, etc., a girlfriend would either tempt me to neglect more important things, or the relationship would cut off immediately. Maybe you haven't instilled these ideas in your kids' minds at such a young age as I was. That's okay. Try and start now, and pinpoint exactly what the cause is.

Now that I've outlined the various struggles and consequences of dating, here is how you can help your children avoid dating or to terminate a current relationship.

10-13-year-olds: If you haven't had the "birds and the bees" conversation with them, now is the time to do it. I'm being totally serious here. Now, you don't have to go full commando and dissect every consequence of dating, bringing up numerous statistics, and scaring them out of having any friends at all. What you can do is be a kind, loving father or mother. If you notice your tween making some questionable decisions, and you are suspicious that they might be headed down the road of high school dating, pull them aside and talk to them. Are there any girls/boys they like? Is there anybody they want to become better friends with? They probably won't be honest with you, but if you appear approachable and honest enough, they'll eventually open up. Is there a reason you suspect your tween or teen is hiding secrets from you? It might be that they're scared to tell you; afraid you'll get mad. If they feel guilty about something, whether it be dating or another struggle, and they timidly open up to you about it, be forgiving and soft. Commend them on their honesty. When it comes to the dating question, encourage them to make new friends but not to become obsessed with a single person. Unlock diversity in their life, not exclusivity.

14-18-year-olds: These are the critical years. Studies say that the majority of life decisions are already decided by age 11-13, but these are the years when your kids start acting them out. You really have to start preaching anti-dating and the importance of it. If you have to, buy a D.A.D.D. shirt (Dads Against Daughters Dating). My dad, who is a youth pastor, has spoken on the importance of keeping yourself pure during high school many a time, to me, my family, and our youth group. If you do the same, you will have a much higher percentage of keeping your son/daughter out of a high school dating relationship.

So here is what I challenge you to do: if you haven't had that important conversation, do it as soon as possible. My parents, when I was 9-11 years old had the 'birds and bees' conversation. Then as I got older, they started talking about dating, their thoughts about it, and poured their wisdom into me. Thanks to them, I am committed and determined not to open myself up to another girl until I'm ready. Start that conversation with your child.

Keep in mind, this isn't a one-time talk with your teen. It is an ongoing conversation. Bring it up once in a while and ask questions. If your teen is already dating, determine the cause. Have they told you yet, or did you do some snooping and stumble upon the evidence? It they told you, at least they are being honest. If they haven't, then you know it can get serious soon. Act immediately. Talk to them about it. If they turn defensive and make excuses or get angry, remain calm and attentive. Pray to God that he would reveal a plan of action to you.

Let me leave you with this idea: If David, the man after God's own heart, Samson, the strongest of them all, and Solomon, the wisest of them all, couldn't keep themselves from impurity and sexual temptation, what makes you think your teen can? Help your teen stay pure. Keep them from sexual immorality. Have you done your job? Start today.

I mentioned that instead of dating, your teen should focus on building healthy friendships with their Godly friends. In this next chapter, Cayden will share more on how to do that.

FRIENDS

"When we honestly ask ourselves which person in our lives mean the most to us, we often find that it is those who, instead of giving advice, solutions, or cures, have chosen rather to share our pain and touch our wounds with a warm and tender hand. The friend who can be silent with us in a moment of despair or confusion, who can stay with us in an hour of grief and bereavement, who can tolerate not knowing, not curing, not healing and face with us the reality of our powerlessness, that is a friend who cares."

— Henri Nouwen

Friends and Influence

Friends can decide what the outline of your life is going to be. Friends will be the greatest influence in your teenager's life. Friends have an influence and all reading this book know this. If your teen is hanging out with individuals that are selfish and want attention and do not care about the heart of your son/daughter, it is time for you to step in and remove them. My parents tell me they are my authority, and they are held accountable for my actions and what I am exposed to, so they are constantly in my business with friends. Have you asked your teen what they are looking for in a friend? What qualities are important to them? If not, put this book down and answer these questions. The teens pressure is to hang out with the popular crowd. Then the pressure increases when the "in crowd" wants your teen to partake in their activities. 1st Corinthians says it best: "Do not be deceived, bad company ruins good morals". This truth clearly states that your teen will become their environment. A friend that will encourage your teen and give them confidence is the kind of friend you are helping find for them. Qualities that I look for in a friend are how they act around parents, their spiritual beliefs, and their attitude. When you encourage friends with the above-mentioned qualities, you are leading boldly in setting the tone of your teens influence. It is important that your teen has a strong foundation, so when they are swayed in their events, beliefs, and attitude, they will stay strong. I suggest that you, parent/guardian, create an environment where friends want to come to your teens house so that you can monitor and model healthy relationships. Proverbs 27:6 says, "Wounds from a sincere friend is better than many kisses from an enemy." I believe this Scripture leads us in the type of true, positive friendships we need to seek and ones not afraid to be real when we are getting off course.

The Right Friends

Friends, in my opinion, are in the top three of the greatest influencers along with family and music. What I see leaving my generation in friends are ones instilling in each other courage, hope, and purpose. The right friends bring out the good in you. Qualities I have been taught to seek from my parents are: belief in Jesus Christ above everything else, kind and loving to all company they are around, and not just a "click," stays away from trouble, ones who give you confidence, and friends that set a good example by how they talk and live their life. My parents have always said how other teens I am engaging with treat their families will say a lot about whether or not I need to go into this friendship. My parents are also big on how we treat our own brother and sister, which is another sign if this will be a healthy relationship. I had a friend who was so cool when he was around parents and me; but when my brother and his friend were around, there was a sudden change. "Good friends care for each other, close friends understand each other, but true friends stay forever beyond words, beyond distance, beyond time." - unknown

The Wrong Friends

Possibly, the most important decision involving relationships your teen will make is discerning the right friend. My dad is an administrator of a high school full of eleven hundred students. He comes home every day with a story of someone doing the wrong thing because of his or her friend group. Many of these students were on the right track with grades, but the wrong attention from the wrong friends lead to failing in school and other activities they were involved in. Are you noticing any of these areas beginning to lack because of your teen's peer groups? Start early helping your teen make good friend choices because it will help when they are out of the house, in college or vocation, be drawn to the right friends, and will continue to live out the morals, principles, and beliefs you have taught them. Proverbs 14:6-7 states, "A scoffer seeks wisdom and finds none, but knowledge is easy to one who has understanding. Leave the presence of a fool, or you will not discern words of knowledge" (Proverbs 14:6-7). A few take-away's from bad friendships are: cheaters accuse you of cheating, liars accuse you of lying and insecure people make you feel insecure. It is your responsibility as the guardian to bring this to the light. Discernment of your teens friends is what I see as one of the top qualities of parenting teenagers.

Practical Application

The 10 Essential Friendship Traits:

1. I am trustworthy.

2. I am honest with others.

3. I am generally very dependable.

4. I am loyal to the people I care about.

5. I am easily able to trust others.

6. I experience and express empathy for others.

7. I am able to be non-judgmental.

8. I am a good listener.

9. I am supportive of others in their good times

10. I am supportive of others in their bad times.

Now, my brother Jackson will talk about the outgoing teenager. He will encourage you to help your teen get out of their comfort zone and be different among their generation.

YOUR OUTGOING TEEN

If only two percent of the two billon Christians in the world would care for a single orphan in distress, there would effectively be no more orphans. If everybody would be willing to simply do something to care for one of these precious treasures, I think we would be amazed by just how much we could change the world.

Every parent hopes to raise an outgoing teen with good personal, relational, and social skills, but I am coming at a different angle with your outgoing teen. Literally, one that "goes out" and lives with an open hand to serve, not a closed hand living only for themselves.

How We Can Help the Orphans

Is it not to share your food with the hungry and to provide the poor wanderer with shelter— when you see the naked, to clothe them, and not to turn away from your own flesh and blood? – Isaiah 58:7

Every Monday for over a year, my mom would have to drive thirty minutes one way to take our foster kids to their parent visit, which consisted of the kids in a room with their parents for a few hours. After that, she would hurry home and homeschool us. Do you think that my mom would look forward to Monday? Not exactly. Why? It separated her from her family just so the kids could have a little time to see their parents. Why do we foster? Every one of those foster kids did not choose to have abusive, neglectful, or drug addicted parents. Orphan's did not ask to leave their home's. This is where we come in. We have the privilege to offer a safe home for kids who have never been taught manners or how to carry on a conversation. Yes, some days are worse than others, but in the end, it is totally worth it. To see a kid through until the day of their adoption or the day they are reunified with their families brings it full circle why we care for orphans. I do not know if your heart has been tugged to foster or adopt, but this is one of the most selfless and sacrificial acts of love you and your teen could experience. Respite care, which is watching a foster child, for a short time period, is another way you and your teen can get involved with the orphan. One of the many reasons people do not foster is they know they could get attached to the child, and they could possibly go home. However, we have learned, as you would, it is not about us; it's about them. We have a family of five, but as of recently, we became a family of eight after the adoption of three siblings. By stepping out, I have learned a greater lesson about not making life about me. Here are three points on how to begin fostering: 1. Pray for God's direction, whether to foster through CPS or an agency. 2. Become certified through the organization you choose. 3 Wait and pray for the Lord to bring a child into your home, and just trust God as you navigate your journey.

Find Others in Need

For you have been a stronghold to the poor, a stronghold to the needy in his distress, a shelter from the storm and a shade from the heat; for the breath of the ruthless is like a storm against a wall.- Isaiah 25:4.

If your teen knows someone in school who is lonely or depressed, ask your teen to do something about it. Most of us judge unfairly. Think about the Good Samaritan, who chose not only to stop and help the person in need but went the extra mile to help. Recognition is a word my dad has taught me that applies to every situation in life. Finding others in need is about recognizing what is going on around us. I have gone to a laundromat with my family with a bag of quarters to fill machines as a random act of kindness. After hearing about a F-5 tornado that tore through parts of Alabama, we left Texas with a few other families to help anyone in need. We regularly help the homeless that we see and pray for those with needs greater than ours is a high priority in our home. Loving your neighbor as yourself is equal to the greatest commandment. Model for your teen, and include them in placing the needs of others first and foremost. Your teens see what you do, and they will follow. So, when your teen sees you pass that homeless man at the red light, they will do the same. Teach your teen to love the homeless and needy; so later in life, they will help the helpless. Instill in your teen the passion of finding ones in need, so this will become routine in their life.

Supporting No Matter What

Some of your teen's ideas may seem crazy, like wanting to take a trip overseas. I can understand where you would wonder where you are going to get the funds. You may even ask, How can we possibly make this happen? Then you're like, where are we going to get that kind of money? Challenge your teen with this task because teens rarely think things through such as purchases and what it takes to pull off a big trip. If you and your teen do not have the means to go to the needy parts of the world, help your teen support a child overseas that would never have a chance. We do this through Compassion International. Support the idea that your teen wants to make a difference. Engage with your teen by encouraging them to support a mission trip your local church is going on or one they have heard about. The reason for lack of wanting to help is teens do not have support. Most teens go home from school to an empty house where idle time takes hold and the motivation to "do something" is drained out of them. Help your teen dream, and encourage them to do hard things. Jay Strack the founder of Student Leadership University says, "The future belongs to those who are prepared."

Loving Blind

"The only rock I know that stays steady, the only institution I know that works, is the family". - Lee Iacocca

When we got our first foster kid, it was not love at first sight. We thought it would be, but it wasn't. We all are like that; we just want our own perfect little world. But Isaiah 1:17 tells us that it is our duty to take care off the ones who are uncared for. That is why, even though we were not immediately in love with our new baby, we would grow to love her because we are called to love no matter what. We protect ourselves by not clinging to them, and that is not a God thing.

We need to love blindly. We need to love like Jesus did. No one wanted to be around the sick and the hurting except Him. If you could instill in your teen to love blindly and have faith like a child, our generation would be so much better. There would not be half the orphans in the world. Fostering is awesome for me because I get to impact a child's life by giving them a fresh start. Yes, some days we question why we do this, but most days are cool to watch the kids grow. If you do not feel like you can open your home, support a child overseas as I have mentioned in a previous paragraph. There is always a way to help. I personally like to interact with kids and play with them. My sister is great with babies, and my brother is also good with kids. My mom always says she could not do without us. If we would just love no matter how someone looks, smells, or sounds, we as teens would understand our purpose much earlier in life. If there is a kid at school that is different, tell your teen to go talk to him. Maybe, they can become friends. You would think that parents would love more blindly, but I do not see this kind of selfless love much. Parents put up walls of comfort; but when you allow ones in need to cross the barrier, they usually get attached. Most people do not foster because they will get attached and must let the kid go home. Trust me it happened, and it was not cool, but the fact that I got to be a part of change in that kids' life is awesome. You would think that everyone would want to do something, but people just seem to not "have the time," or worse, they are too comfortable.

Practical Application

Here are some ways to help your teen be more outgoing.

1. Get your teens more involved with mission work. This will help them not be afraid to share the Word of God.

2. Community service activities like reading to children after school, volunteering to babysit kids with special needs, and mentoring kids that don't have good influences.

3. Have them get up and speak in front of people, so they will be more comfortable when talking to others.

Cayden will now bring encouragement to a new light and will brighten your outlook as he presents the gift of encouragement in the next chapter.

The Gift of Encouragement

One day, a man went to visit a church. He arrived early, parked his car, and got out. Another car pulled up near him, and the driver told him, "I always park there. You took my place!"

The visitor went inside for Sunday School, found an empty seat, and sat down. A young lady from the church approached him and stated, "That's my seat! You took my place!"

The visitor was somewhat distressed by this rude welcome, but said nothing.

After Sunday School, the visitor went into the church sanctuary and sat down. Another member walked up to him and said, "That's where I always sit. You took my place!"

The visitor was even more troubled by this treatment, but still said nothing.

Later, as the congregation was praying for Christ to dwell among them, the visitor stood, and his appearance began to change.

Horrible scars became visible on his hands and on his sandaled feet. Someone from the congregation noticed him and called out, "What happened to you?"

The visitor replied, "I took your place."

How important is it to you to speak encouraging words? You may never know who you are speaking too or the situation they are in.

Encouragement to the Depressed

Let me start by mentioning signs of depression you might be seeing in your teen:

1. Isolation

2. Anxiety

3. Always in a bad mood, never happy

4. Chronic Fatigue

5. A low self-esteem, not motivated to do anything

6. Constant feeling of hopelessness

These are just a few signs of depression. Isolation is a major sign something is not right, as our age is typically active. It seems the greatest diagnosis of our generation is anxiety. Encouragement can be great medicine for your teen if you are seeing anxiety. I saw an anonymous quote that stated, "Anxiety is contemplating life without God". It seems many teens are getting worked up over little things, and getting more frustrated and upset. Bad moods, anger, and lack of joy are signs that your teen does not want to be involved or could be involved in things you would not approve. Do you sense your teen is involved in something that would end up discouraging him/her? Also, not being pleasant to be around could cause loss of friendships because of a negative attitude. Encouragement is daily medicine for your teen. "A joyful heart is good medicine, but a crushed spirit dries up the bones" (Proverbs 17:22). What part of this Scripture best describes your teen? How are you encouraging a joyful heart?

Chronic fatigue is another sign that seems to be affecting more and more teens. I know I feel lazy and sluggish when I have long school days, anxiety over projects, and tiring activities through the week, and it helps when I can hear encouraging words that pick me up. A low self-esteem in teenagers is an increasing problem. The suicide rate in teens is now at an all-time high. All people reading this book have more than likely been through the physical and emotional change that can be hard to deal with through the teenage years. Do not let up on how you discipline and make extra efforts to increase words of encouragement. The last thing you want for your teen is a feeling of hopelessness, like no one loves them. Encouragement from you reassures them that there is hope in the middle of their struggles.

Encouragement to the Timid

Teenage insecurity can cause one to become timid. Signs your teen is battling timidity:

1. Trouble talking in front of people

2. No confidence

3. Lack of support

4. Feel left out

"Let no corrupting talk come out of your mouths, but only such as is good for building up, as fits the occasion, that it may give grace to those who hear" (Ephesians 4:29). We need to make sure that what we are saying is building people up not breaking them down. I know plenty of teens and parents who are timid. Parents/Guardians, if you are shy, chances are your child will struggle with this. I am not shy, and it is because my parents encourage me to do things out of my comfort zone. My parents have encouraged me to stand up in front of our church when fundraising, and they encourage me to pray aloud in prayer meetings. I am also required to speak weekly at the co-op I attend, which is hard because it is a small group in front of my peers. I can tell you from experience, there will have to be an extra nudge to get them to take advantage of speaking opportunities. I attend leadership conferences that help build my skills in the area of encouragement. A lack of confidence often comes from a lack of encouragement by peers and families.

What is the communication level between you and your teen? Are there barriers? Does your teen share with you the hard things they are going through that lead or pull to negative behaviors?

The two greatest influences of our age are peers and music. Are these two areas encouraging your teen? I would encourage you to build a relationship with your teen that encourages open conversations, especially in the area of peers and music. I used to have "dead man" talks with my dad; where during that specific moment I could tell him anything, and he could not react to the situation with any emotion. This created an open line of communication between my father and I. Confident, encouraged teens have a greater chance resisting the things that come into their lives that will have a negative impact. Many teens feel left out, and teens have created this life because their parents have not pushed them out of their comfort zone. I am not blaming all the parents because the kids must have the desire to step out and stretch themselves in communicating with and in front of people.

The Influence Encouragement Has on Other People

There is great power in encouragement, and the influence it has on people is tangible. In the last five years, we went on mission trips to Alaska, Alabama, Oklahoma, and other places. On the Alabama trip, there was an F5 tornado that wiped out the places we went to, and they seemed hopeless. We were there to help restore the community and give them hope. Once we got there, the people were so scared, and their homes were destroyed. People said it sounded like a freight train coming at their house. We did all that we could to help, prayed over them, and encouraged them in rebuilding their lives. It is so important for your teen to get their hands dirty with people rather than just hearing or seeing struggles. I would heavily encourage your teen to go on mission trips, or find ones to encourage in your community. As I have said in another chapter, is your teen an asset or liability?

Reaching out to influence others is something all of us can do, and it builds our confidence. "Therefore, encourage one another and build one another up, just as you are doing" (1 Thessalonians 5:11).

Practical Application

5 ways to encourage others:

1. Encourage the smallest effort. It may seem small, but to the one who has performed the task, recognition is a big deal!

2. Stop finding fault with the wrong, and applaud the right.

3. Look for outwardly demonstrable ways to encourage a person. Stars or happy faces work with children. Badges, certificates and gifts, and notes works better for older people.

4. Do not respond to negative words or actions. Instead, combat the negative with positive comments and body language.

5. Make positive comments. It is very important to give positive feedback, not negative.

Jackson, in the next chapter. will discuss the power confession has and the things you can do to help your teen be a man/woman of confession.

How to Destroy the Root of All Sin

Every sin starts somewhere. Where does yours begin? What about your teen? Sin is buried in lie after lie. This is where you come in as a parent to help navigate your teen through the recognition of their sin. Sin is destroyed by becoming a man and woman of confession and letting go of your burdens. Teach submission to God and humility, so your teen will open up to you about their struggles.

Confession

To confess is to open your heart and lay every sin, thoughts, words, and actions at the feet of Jesus. This is exactly why Jesus was slain. God gave his one and only son, so that when trouble comes, He will relieve your every burden.

Do your kids look up to you? Do you like your job? Do you and your teen communicate well? Are you weary? The answer to these questions will play a big part in helping destroy the root of sin in your teen. If you're hurting and broken within, tell someone. You will need a place to release before you can help your teen. My parents are my go-to when I need to talk about burdensome things. Does your teen have someone to talk to?

The best tool in the parental tool belt, in my opinion, is communication. Does your teen have an open line of communication with you? If your teen is struggling with sin, or having issues outside of home, who are they talking to? Nurturing relationships in your teen's life with people of accountability will benefit them greatly as they get older. Guide them to always have someone to talk to, like your pastor, family, mentors, or you. Pastors, close family, and mentors are relationships that your teen can develop that allow them someone they can confess to. Satan wants you and your teen to keep sin in the dark.

Having healthy relationships nurtures the soil of confession. To hide sin is to play on Satan's playground. Ephesians 5:13 states," But their evil intentions will be exposed when the light shines on them." The root of all sin is pride, which keeps your teen from confession, so as the Scripture says, bring it to the light! Depression is increasing amongst teens, and lying still has a stronghold on our generation. The solution is confession and our God redeems and renews that which the enemy has stolen, through confession. Confession, which leads to repentance, is the key ingredient that Satan hates because it destroys the root of all sin.

How to Train Your ~~Dragon~~ Teen

"The family should be a closely-knit group. The home should be a shelter of security; a kind of school where God is honored: a place where wholesome recreation and simple pleasures are enjoyed. -**Billy Graham**

Reading challenging subjects with your teen and having them memorize Scripture will only enhance the family environment. That is what my mom has continued through our teenage years. So, doing challenging things is very important. Regarding training, do you drop your teen off at Sunday school, or youth group? What does your teen get out of their fellowship time? Do they talk about what they are learning at fellowship or about what happened at school? Remember, you are your teen's greatest trainer. You need to be in the middle of seeing and hearing what your teen is seeing and hearing. A great training tool is worship with other believers. It has been modeled for me to sit and listen to the word whoever is teaching. You go to church to celebrate, fellowship, and worship the God who has given every breath you have breathed just as you have been reading this book. I have visited a church where in the Sunday School, there was more focus on iPads and Xbox's than the word of God. I am sorry if I am stepping on toes, but this is not the church that I read about in Acts.

Our age group does not need any more screen time to fill time or distract from true worship. Good training also comes by eating together at the table. Spending time with your teen in meaningful conversation will open up more opportunities for them to talk. Training your teen starts with you modeling what you want them to become. An Olympian's strongest training session occurs when no one is watching. Be intentional with your training in your home. Like the gold medal Olympian, you will be able to celebrate the victory your teen has over sin.

Help Your Teen

When you put faith hope, and love together, you can raise positive kids in a negative world.

-Zig Ziglar.

One way to help your teen is to talk to them about their struggles and hardships. Listen and look intently to see what distractions cause struggles and hardships. It seems the number one distraction is their phone. The phone is possibly their best friend. Some might even say that they can't live without it. False. The only thing we cannot live without is Jesus Christ. The reason your teen hides things is because of who their friends are. Help your kids choose their friends, particularly, ones who are polite and caring. What are your kids doing at school? Do you know? Most teens would rather be around their friends than they would be around their parents. Why? Their parents are not showing the attention that the teens want, or the teens do not care about their family's and want to do whatever they want. My parents are raising us in a balanced home. I like hanging out with my friends and playing sports, but I also like hanging around the fire with my family. Just being there for your teen helps build trust, so they will communicate what he or she truly feels. Help your teen destroy the root of all sin by being intentional and involved in every area of his or her life.

Quality Time

Spend quality time with your children to make them feel loved, wanted, and build their self-esteem up, so when they go out into the world with confidence. -**Nishan Panwar.**

Spending quality time together as a family is invaluable and sets the tone for the days and weeks ahead. This also gives a standard to meet when they have a family. My family and I love to read a book or memorize Scripture together. We love the true stories of ones who have lived hard things and challenged themselves to make a difference in this life. My parents challenge us to be different and not fit in with the herd, and to be excellent in how we live. We have contests who can memorize Scripture first; and sometimes, the winner gets a prize. Those are things that encouraged us to stay connected to God. Quality time like this with your teen helps destroy the root of sin in their life. God gave you as the authority over your children to help them in all areas of their life. Quality family time helps uncover the sin that has been covered in lies. To spend time together is a way to stay bonded and it develop the trust between parents and child that allows for real conversation. Quality time brings out kindness in your teen, which combats sin. My mom tells us, "If you can't treat the people in your family with kindness, then you won't be able to treat those in the world with kindness". My dad, who is a principal at a high school, says that most teens that are in trouble usually do not have two parents that spend time with them. Love no matter what, whether life is easy or hard. Love is the answer to your teen discovering their purpose and their cause of their sinful nature known as selfishness. Many parents today are directing their teen to a pill or counseling when quality time is the better prescription. Quality time will play a crucial part in destroying everything that revolves around sin, and you will see the fruit of your parenting come out in your teen through helping and loving others.

Staying Away from Sin

If your teen has a problem and you know what it is, help them remove the struggle. For example, if they are addicted to their phone, remove their phone. Even if you think it's too hard to stop texting, or whatever you battle with, go back to Philippians 4:13. If they are involved in inappropriate social media or simply pulling away from their family, come in to help. Teens want you to hold them accountable and be in their business; they just are not going to admit it. It is part of the parenting job. The aspect of discipline in parenting these days is grounding them or removing a device, but there must be more than this. Parents are here to guide us, so when we get into the real world, we will know how to go about in life. Everyone makes mistakes, so tell your teen this so they will not have the pressure of trying to be perfect. If you have any regrets or you wish you could have done something differently, teach your teen to avoid that same mistake. Going to church, getting your teen involved in youth groups, date nights with your teen, camping trips, nightly conversations are quality things that will help them run the race that God intended. Have good reconciliation with your teens. If you get off track, lax on disciplining them, and lose track of what they are doing, reconcile by being honest about your failure to engage. Reunite with your teen and target his or her weakness, and help your teen strengthen that part. Avoid sin, attack Satan, and lean in on your teen's hardships, and help them succeed. Yes, there are hard times, but you can overcome them by the grace of God. John 3:16 says God gave His one and only son, and we cannot stop looking down at our phones instead of looking up at God. This requires intentional parenting, praying, and continuing the fight for their heart during hard times.

Practical Applications

1. Reward the Truth

As parents, we are often quick to scold. Sometimes we aren't always so quick to praise. Reward honesty with loads of praise and hugs. It will build self-confidence and reinforce positive behavior. Plus, a child can never get too much love.

2. Speak the Truth

Teach your kids that they don't have to give false compliments. If they don't have a kind word to say, teach them how to control their words and not say anything. However, we should always be able to find something positive to say about anyone.

3. Say the Hard Truth

Speaking truth is more important than avoiding hurting someone's feelings who is out of line. Wrong is always wrong. For instance, your son's best friend is cheating on tests and your son is fully aware. He has a duty to go to his friend and advise him to quit. He's hurting himself and cheating the others who have honestly studied. If he refuses, then your son would have to tell the teacher about what is going on. That is the hard truth.

4. Model the Truth

"When we get in the habit of telling small lies, it leads to a habit of telling big ones."

As is always the case, you are the role model. You do not want your child to hear you telling a lie. Live by the truth. If your children see you telling even "harmless" white lies, they will feel like it's ok to lie as well. When we get in the habit of telling small lies, it leads to a habit of telling big ones. Put thought and initiative into telling and seeking the truth all the time.

5. Don't Put Them to the Test

Though it's tempting to test them, try to avoid asking questions that give your child a chance to not be honest. You saw your daughter spill red juice on the couch. No need to ask, "Did you just spill your juice on the couch?" This leads her to believe she might have a way out and possibly could pass blame elsewhere. Just tell her to clean it up. She'll have enough opportunities to tell the truth.

The next chapter was written by Zach, who talks about the benefits of a healthy father/son relationship and why this is crucial for your teens journey.

Good Dad, Great Dad

Before reading this chapter, I want to pose a question to you: Of what importance do you view your relationship with your kids? Think about it. Be honest. Pray and ask God to reveal how important it is to you. Then, I want you to evaluate your answer. Out of ten, is it a nine? Eight? Five?

"Well Zach, I love my kids, but my job takes up most of my day, and I've got my buddies to hang out with, and I'm just way too busy."

"To be honest, my relationship with my kids has been rocky as of late, and I don't know how to reconnect with them."

"Well, I love my kids, and I know I need to spend more time with them, but I just can't find the time."

"Zach, I'm proud to say that I love my kids more than anything else on this earth (aside from my wife,) and I couldn't be more thankful."

No matter your response, I believe you'll find something in this chapter to make your fatherhood adventure more interesting, or maybe realize you were missing something. Now that you've established your position, realize that you may have to change. Keep that in your mind as you continue reading.

Let's go.

What Is the Problem?

On October 15, 1992, an article came out in the *Bits and Pieces* magazine, stating, "There's a Spanish story of a father and son who had become estranged. The son ran away, and the father set off to find him. He searched for months to no avail. Finally, in a last desperate effort to find him, the father put an ad in a Madrid newspaper. The ad read: 'Dear Paco, meet me in front of this newspaper office at noon on Saturday. All is forgiven. I love you. Your Father.' On Saturday, eight hundred Paco's showed up, looking for forgiveness and love from their fathers." (p.13)

This is one of countless stories that demonstrates the circumstances that our current world is living in. Thousands, possibly even millions of families are left without fathers, whether by estrangement, divorce/separation, or death. Statistics show us that there are millions of children in the U.S. without a father, and the number of ways they are affected is truly staggering. Here are some of those statistics:

As of 2017, according to the U.S. Census Bureau, 19.7 million children (more than one in four) live without a father in the home. Those children and families are affected in the following ways:

- Four times greater risk of living in poverty

- 7x more likely to become pregnant as a teen

- 2x greater risk of infant mortality

- 2x more likely to suffer obesity

- 2x more likely to drop out of high school

- More likely to have behavioral problems, face child abuse and neglect, abuse drugs and alcohol, commit crime and go to prison (Statistics provided by National Fatherhood Initiative®).

- According to the US Department of Health/Census, 63% of youth suicides are from fatherless homes—five times the average.

- 90% of all homeless and runaway children are from fatherless homes (Thefatherlessgeneration.wordpress.com).

Yeah, it's that bad. As my pastor would say, chew on that.

Now, chew some more.

Once you are done chewing, continue reading.

Ready to go? Let's dive back in.

The Father is the leader of the home, both physically and spiritually. When the father is not present, correction and discipline crumble. "Young men who grow up in homes without fathers are twice as likely to end up in jail as those who come from traditional two-parent families...those boys whose fathers were absent from the household had double the odds of being incarcerated -- even when other factors such as race, income, parent education and urban residence were held constant." (Harper & McLanahan)

The evidence is all around. When fathers are absent, families' and children's lives become the devil's playground. If you have been estranged from your children, or if you've been neglecting them, be bold. Turn back and save your children's livelihood—before it's too late. Even if you and your kids aren't at this stage yet, never slack off. If you are sensing even a slight rift between you and your children, act immediately. Your kids need you to be there for them, praying before meals, playing fun games, or teaching them practical life lessons. Don't just be there to eat, then go off to bed to finish your work, then miss out on putting them to bed. Do more. Tuck them in. Read them a bedtime story, or tell them one. Are they too old for that? If they are, have some honest conversations with them about their life (school, friends, family, cute girls, cute boys, etc.); and always, always, pray that God will renew your relationship daily with your family.

Good Dad vs. Great Dad

But wait! I can hear you. "I'm there for my kids. I'm not leaving them for drugs or for crime. I'm not abandoning my wife and leaving my kids to fend for themselves. I'm a good dad!"

Oh, I believe you. Those statements were placed there just to show you, as a faithful, loving father and husband (hopefully), how well you are doing compared to the other thousands of fathers who are throwing away their family and livelihood for drugs and money.

Yes, you are a good dad. But 'good' isn't going to cut it. To change the upcoming generation, your children will need *great* leadership and influence in their lives, *great* inspiration and motivation implanted in their minds, *great* life lessons to take away and apply, and *great* love and affection poured out on them. A good dad plays when his kids ask him; a great dad asks his kids to play. A good dad prays for his kids; a great dad teaches his kids how to pray. A good dad shows up to his kid's games; a great dad encourages his kid, analyzes the game to death, and embarrasses even the soccer moms by shouting, groaning, and cheering for his child. So, if you asked your kids today if you were a good dad, would they respond with 'yes!' or 'you're a great dad!' As a matter of fact, why don't you do that right now? Put down this book and find out what your kids really think about you.

First, ask if you're a good dad. Most likely, your child will respond with 'yes!' right off the bat. Ask them why. They will tell you. They will most likely finish with 'I love you!' Tell them you love them back, then act like the conversation has ended. Then ask them if you are a great dad. Try to get a little more in depth at this point in the conversation. Sure, it'll be challenging and (Dare I say it to a fearless, strong man like you?) scary, but be open with them. If you haven't been the dad you have the potential to be, and you know it, tell them what you've been doing, and share with them what you need to do to become better. Most importantly, be open to your kid's criticism. If they are shy at first or afraid of embarrassing you, coax them out of that mode. Ask them to be honest. Ask them what you need to do to become a great dad.

Listen to what they have to say. Once they're done, write down what you learned. Then, come back and continue reading.

Did the results surprise you? Challenge you? Strengthen you? Whatever feeling you received after having that conversation, embrace it. If you were challenged, let that challenge motivate you to become better. If it strengthened you, let that strength fill you up and help you to continue doing the right thing.

If for some reason you didn't talk to your kids, or you weren't able to, that's totally okay. If you were scared or just too lazy, talk to your wife. C'mon, you can't say you don't have time to talk to your wife about your family. Ask her if there is anything you could be doing better. Ask her if there is anything you *both* could be doing better. Be open. If you can't be this open with your wife, ask God to give you the strength to have this conversation. After the conversation is over, pray together for your family and thank God for the opportunity to minister and mentor your kids.

If you did one of the two or both of the suggestions above, then kudos to you. You are headed on the right track, but it's not over yet. It's not a "one time" thing. It's a daily decision, to step up and lead your family the way it deserves. Continue to pray and be open with your family. If you want to go above and beyond, then have some accountability partners to pray with you, encourage you and sharpen you. Find some guys that you trust and look up to, like a close friend, a pastor, a mentor, or your dad (You are NEVER too old to ask him for help).

This is why I am writing this chapter: A) So you can be encouraged that you're not doing as bad as some people (You've stayed faithful and true to your wife and your kids,) and B) to challenge you from being just an okay, average, Mr. Jones-type father to the A-plus, best possible version of the dad you can be.

What Does the Bible Say?

Proverbs 17:6b states, "Parents are the pride of their children." Are you the pride of your kid's life? I sure know that my mom and dad are. My mom has been homeschooling my two sisters and me since the 1st grade, and she also leads the 11th graders at our homeschool group, Classical Conversations. My dad now works as an administrator at Tyler Junior College and is currently working on his Doctorate in Education. He is also the youth pastor of my home church, and I get the privilege (not obligation) of hearing him speak every Sunday and Wednesday. They have taught me almost everything I know and have led me and helped me grow in every area of my life. They are the pride of my life. What about you? Are you the pride of your children's life?

Ephesians 4:6 states, "Fathers, do not provoke your children to anger, but bring them up in the discipline and instruction of the Lord." Colossians 3:21 speaks a similar message, "Fathers, do not provoke your children, lest they become discouraged." This is a big one. Are you provoking your children? Probably not in the way that you would think, but are your sarcastic comments, quippy lines, and indifferent brush-offs of your children or your wife discouraging them? Or, are you bringing them up in the discipline and instruction of the Lord? If you have been unwittingly provoking your children, it's time to change. Let this verse become your new foundation.

Proverbs 13:24 says, "Whoever spares the rod hates their children, but the one who loves their children is careful to discipline them." This verse is all about discipline. You can't be lax when it comes to your children's behavior. You can't check out and simply not care about who they date, what they listen to, or what they read or watch. You need to be kind and loving, but also firm and authoritative. No abusing your power though! You're not a tyrant, but you *are* their daddy. You care for them and want what's best for them. Enacting boundaries and curfews aren't tyranny; it's a responsibility.

Now, I know what you're thinking. These verses are very simple and easy to understand. Every dad knows how to do these things (Or, how not to!) Well, if you thoroughly understand the concepts and the teachings in these verses, then you have already built the foundation of a successful fatherhood. But many, many fathers have not mastered these keys to a fruitful fatherhood, and that is why more and more kids today are being thrust into bouts of depression, loss, and are turning more and more to crime, drugs, you name it. If you are a father who has neglected your responsibilities, and has struggled with your relationships with your kids, guess what? It's not too late. Here are some recommended books on growing as a father: *The Father Connection* by Josh McDowell, *Parenting* by Paul David Tripp, and *Shepherding a Child's Heart* by Tedd Tripp. I highly encourage struggling fathers or first-time fathers to read these books.

The number one key to having a wonder-filled fatherhood is fear of the Lord. It talks about it in Psalm 128, which is a Psalm written to fathers. It states, "How joyful are those who fear the Lord—all who follow his ways! You will enjoy the fruit of your labor; how joyful and prosperous you will be! Your wife will be like a fruitful grapevine, flourishing within your home. Your children will be like vigorous young olive trees as they sit around your table. This is the blessing for those who fear him."

Flourishing! Those who fear the Lord are constantly growing and flourishing in the grace of God. Everything will be affected—your work, your wife, your children, your life, all of it! No matter how little you have, or how much you have, you constantly cling to God and His promise upon your life: *I will ALWAYS be with you*. That is what it looks like to be a great, loving, kind father.

Luke 15 talks about the prodigal son; a story I'm sure you're familiar with. But, I believe it can work the other way too. If you have become a prodigal father, if you have run off and done your own thing, forgetting your family, or if you just haven't been there enough, there is no better time than now to repent. Malachi 4:6b says, "His preaching will turn the hearts of fathers to their children, and the hearts of children to their fathers." Repent and seek forgiveness, both from

God and your family. Continue to ask God to help you and strengthen you, and he will answer your prayers.

Speaking of prayer, in the next chapter Jackson will discuss strategies for your teen's prayer life. Who knows, maybe even you'll learn something new!

Walking From Death to Life

Jesus taught us how to pray, so we must take heed and listen. Everything I will be talking about I have learned from experiences in just these few years. For example, my family and I go to a prayer meeting every Wednesday. We eat, fellowship, worship, and usually spend one solid hour of praying. One time as I was praying, I heard someone say "amen," and after church the person came up to me and said that it was a good prayer. I realized that I was praying to impress people more than communicating with the Father. Praying to get that amen and not focusing on talking to God will hinder your relationship with Him. Jesus taught on this in Luke 18:10-14. Our focus needs to be vertical, which leads to humility, not horizontal, which exalts ourselves.

Don't Pray to Impress

Matthew 6:1 "Be careful not to practice your righteousness in front of others to be seen by them. If you do, you will have no reward from your Father in heaven.

Does your family pray at the dinner table? If so, are your family members praying because of eating quicker, or are they giving thanks that they have food? If prayer means getting to food faster, ask yourself this question: Who provided your food? Are you modeling for your teen thankfulness to God for his provision? Instill in your teen that He took his time creating them, blessing them, so it is important they take the time to thank Him. I have to admit I have been guilty of praying with the wrong motivation many times. Emphasize to your teenager the importance of taking time every day to talk to God. It does not have to be long, just with the right heart.

Favor Comes from God by Spending Time with God

"To have God speak to the heart is a majestic experience, an experience that many people might miss if they monopolize the conversation and never pause to hear God's response."- Charles Stanley.

Praying may seem to be a small thing, but it is not. As a matter of fact, it is the most powerful thing you can do! In the Bible, God was in control of every battle. In Judges, God gave favor to Gideon, and they won. When God gave favor to David, he won. David defeated a ninefoot giant with all odds against him! He had the favor of God because of the time he spent with him. When God was disappointed with Israel, they were slaughtered. Why? They weren't staying in touch with Him; therefore, it led to their destruction, and they were punished. Teaching your teen that time with God is a top priority will help them manage life's demanding deadlines and distractions.

The number one distraction is idols. I just realized myself that we still have idols today. They just come in different forms. I am not necessarily talking about statues, or hand carved "gods"; I am talking about cellphones, money, music, sports figures, and everything else Satan uses to try to fill our appetite and keep our attention and devotion. The only way your teen can stay away from these things is by staying connected to God through prayer. Tony Evans says it well when he informs, "prayer brings Heaven into history." Praying is time with God and you, it's intimate time with your creator who desires your communication. Matthew 6:33 states, "But seek you first the kingdom of God, and his righteousness; and all these things shall be added unto you". Teaching your teen to seek first the kingdom is teaching them how to experience the favor of God.

Praying Is Talking to God, So Talk to Him as You Would Talk to Your Best Friend

Your talent is God's gift to you. What you do with it is your gift back to God. – Leo Buscaglia

Is praying awkward? Is your teen embarrassed to pray in front of people? I can relate. I was afraid of saying the wrong words or mispronouncing things. It felt very unnatural. Realizing I am not praying for approval of the people, but my Father, changed how I approach prayer. How does your teen talk to his/her earthly father? Is it awkward? Unnatural? Easy? This will probably determine how they talk to the heavenly Father.

 Here's an example of someone who was embarrassed to talk to the One who blessed him. There was a young boy who lived in Africa. His family was extremely poor. Every night he was cold, hungry, and tortured by mosquitoes. There was a businessman who lived in the United States and was very wealthy. One day he felt led to donate money to kids in third world countries, so he received a letter asking if he would like to meet the kid he was donating to, and he jumped at the chance to meet him. At the airport the two met, and the man was excited, but he could not squeeze a word from the kid. The man's heart was crushed. After all he had done for the kid, he didn't say anything. How much more does God bless us even when we don't talk to Him? It is daily, and sadly awkward for us. Teach your teen God is a friend; he is also "Abba" (Daddy) and is not concerned about social or economic status and does not base his relationship on conditions that we humans do.

Speaking Out Loud or In Silence.

For I know the plans I have for you, declares the Lord, plans for welfare and not evil, to give you a future and hope. Then you will hear me and you pray to me and I will hear you. You will seek me and find me when you seek me with all your heart. - Jeremiah 29:11-13

Are you too shy to pray to God out loud? Is your teen too timid when it comes to praying? If so, it's perfectly natural to feel that way. Do not feel like you must pray out loud to be heard. The Lord hears all the time. We are to pray out loud with the intention of speaking to our Lord, not for others to hear. I thought I had to pray out loud, so God could hear me. Paul, in Romans, writes once a believer has the Holy Spirit, He intercedes for you without even speaking a word. *1 John 5:14 reiterates, "This is the confidence we have in approaching God: That if we ask anything according to His will, He hears us."* God is your father, so talk to Him as you would your earthly father. Model for your teen by praying out loud, or by asking them to pray. This will show your teen how impactful praying is, whether it is out loud or quiet. It is important that your teen knows they are praying solely to God because he is the one who can answer it. If your teen wants to pray out loud, encourage Him or Her. If not, that is okay, as long as they are staying in touch with the Father. God cares and wants to hear from them. Whether it's about your struggles or blessings, teach your teen to talk to Him.

Praying Out Loud Has Impact.

Hebrews 5:7 says "While Jesus was here on earth, he offered prayers and pleadings, with a loud cry and tears, to the one who could save him from death. And God heard his prayers because of his deep reverence for God".

Praying out loud is very powerful. It is true that we do not have to pray out loud to be heard by God, but there are major benefits. Encouraging your teen to pray out loud gives them confidence and boldness to continue this into their adulthood. I believe if you as the parent want the standard to serve the Lord established in your home, praying out loud needs to be modeled and encouraged. Praying out loud increases the faith of your teen as they see the powerful change and influence in ones who might be struggling to profess their faith consistently. The reason praying out loud is impactful is that whoever you are praying for will be encouraged and empowered, whether they are sick or fearful, or just hearing the prayer, receives hope and healing. Teach your teen that praying out loud is to block out everything around you and believe in what you are praying for. It gives peace to the restless, strength to the weak, and encouragement to others their age. We all need to speak more life, especially in our generation. *Timothy 3:16-17 claims, "All Scripture is God breathed and is useful for teaching, rebuking, correcting and training in righteousness, so that the servant of God might be thoroughly equipped for every good work."* What pursuit or purpose of your teen could be more noble than that of speaking life into and over others! James 5:16 should empower us to pray for ones when given the opportunity as it says, *"Therefore confess your sins to one another and pray for one another, that you may be healed. The prayer of a righteous person has great power as it is working."*

Conclusion

We have touched on praying not to impress; favor with God is spending time with God, so talk to God as you would a friend, praying out loud and in silence, and how praying out loud is impactful. I would like to share some practical steps your teen can take to stay in touch with God. To mention a few: praying, reading the Bible, surrounding yourself with Godly people, praying for people or asking for prayer, worshiping together, and joining an intentional prayer meeting are experiences I have had to keep me connected and walking in life. I would like to leave you with some quotes from Oswald Chambers that hopefully will impact you like they have me.

"Yet, we refuse to pray unless it thrills or excites us, which is the most intense form of spiritual selfishness."

"There is nothing thrilling about a laboring person's work, but it is the laboring person who makes the ideas of the genius possible. And it is the laboring saint who makes the ideas of his master possible. When you labor in prayer, God always sees a result."

What he is saying is that when you put your hardest effort in your work, there will be a good result. When you are lazy, there is the opposite action. When we pray to God, we need to put real thought into each word; because after all, we are talking to the creator of the world.

Practical Applications

Five prayers based off Jesus' prayer in John 17 (desiringGod.com).

1. Lord, they are yours. "I have manifested your name to the people whom you gave me out of the world. Yours they were and you gave them to me… I am praying for them. I am not praying for the world but those whom you have given me, for they are yours". (John 17: 6-9)

2. Lord, make us one. "Holy Father keep them in your name, that they may be one, even as we are one". (John 17:11)

3. Lord, keep them from evil. "I do not ask that you take them out of the world but you to keep them from the evil one". John (17:15)

4. Lord, give them your joy. "But now I am coming to you and these things I speak to the world, that they may have my joy fulfilled in themselves". John (17:13)

5. Lord, make them holy. "Sanctify them in the truth; your world is truth". (John 17:17)

The next chapter will focus on awakening Monday morning with a smile on your face and an attitude that will bring the best out of your teen.

T.G.I.M Teen

Everyone knows the term "Thank God It's Friday." Almost all grownups and teens I know would rather be at home than at work. Being a teen myself, I understand that Monday morning is not the most exciting morning of the week, but it can be with the right attitude and perspective. Whether it is a job, school, errands, or chores, work does not have to be a burden. Think of it like this, you are working every day for your family, college, or just savings in general for future purchases. Instill in your teenager this mentality and drive each day, so he or she will not only will be able to provide for their own family but will do it with a great attitude. The purpose of our education is to not just get a "good job," but to find a vocation that you love, and one that not only pays the bills and covers everyday expenses, but allows you to impact people and be an influence where you are.

What Are You Doing When No One Else Is Around?

"Live so that when your kids think of fairness and integrity, they think of you."

Your teen's integrity is what he or she is doing at school, on social media, and with friends when you are not around. Do you look through your teen's phone? I know a lot of my friends' parents who do not look through their phones. Phones are, of course, not always a bad thing, but in many cases, they are destructive. This comes down to a seven day a week supervision. Your teen's integrity is based on what he or she is doing when you are not around. Your integrity is based on what you are doing when your teen is around and staying in their business seven days a week. Friends are a big part of your teens life because if we do the math, the majority of teen's spend 2,920 hours together during a school year. I had a friend who was fun to hang out with, and I thought he was a good example, but he started hanging out with worldly friends becoming more addicted to his phone and more negative toward life in general. I Corinthians 15:33 says, "bad company ruins good morals." We need you parents/guardians to live the beginning of the week with the same enthusiasm as you would Friday at five 'o'clock, so our integrity and attitude will stay in check since you are our authority.

Reading the Rule Book

"It's not the amount of Bible you read; it's the amount of Bible you believe and live out."

Think of the Bible as your weekly plumb line, starting your week reading the "guidebook" that helps lead through the narrow gate. Parents who live like this truly look differently than those who never peek into what God has for them to start their week. We need our parents, waking up "thanking God it is Monday," so we will learn to look forward to our day and work no matter what the circumstances are. It is encouraging and helpful to see you spending time with the Lord. On the other hand, I believe the "thank God it's Friday" parent dreads the beginning of the week because their focus is on getting through the day and not enjoying the day and what has been given to them. When all you can look at is Friday, you miss opportunities to disciple or share the "good news" with someone. The TGIF parent shows their teen that the paycheck, vacation, and hobbies are what is worth living for.

I have been fortunate to see my parents reading the Bible and praying for what lies ahead for the day. Seeing this has inspired me and my siblings to do the same. Instill in your teen the love of the Word; so when their friends come around, they will not tell them how many Fortnite eliminations they have, but how many Scriptures they memorized, so they are ready for the real fight.

Jesus taught mostly about what he called the two greatest commandments, "Love the Lord your God with your heart, soul, mind, and strength, and your neighbor as yourself." Focusing on these commandments with your teen will help his or her obedience and help them deny worldly temptations. Teach them the greatest way to bear fruit as a teenager is to obey their parents. I notice when my parents read the Word, a better attitude is created within the entire family. Let me encourage you as you start each week to "Thank God it is Monday".

Your Strongest Weapons

"Spiritual warfare is very real. There is a furious, fierce, ferocious battle raging in the realm of the spirit between the forces of God and the forces of evil. Warfare happens every day, all the time. Whether you believe it or not, you are in a battle field, you are in warfare"- Pedro Okoro

The battle in this chapter we are discussing is a war of drudgery and joy to win the beginning of the week. Victory comes through the weapons of:

Words- Words can build you up, and words can break you down. Build your teen up the minute that alarm goes off. Believe me, I know it is hard to build up when we argue about getting up, but your words are powerful. Proverbs explains, "Life and death lie in the power of the tongue", so speaking life like, "have a great day, I love you, and be excellent today," will spur on your teenager. I have five siblings, three of them are adopted, and I must be careful what I say in case I trigger something from the past. I have experienced both sides, building up, and breaking down; and I know the beginning of my weeks start much better when I hear encouraging words and speak these in return.

Actions- It seems at the start of the week people are looking at your attitudes and body language. We as teens will go through lazy and grumpy phases. I encourage you to help us through with your words and body language. We need support and encouragement; we don't need to be provoked. No one likes to be aggravated, especially when they're already in a bad mood. My experience has been when I am mad or sad, my parents are there for me no matter what the problem is.

They comfort me. When I am sick, my mom is there. When I am struggling in anything, my dad is there to talk. Teens need support, so that every Monday morning will not be a bad thing, but it would be a joy. This will help them win the battle that is going on for our soul.

Putting on the full armor of God- Monday morning is considered by many as the most dreaded day of the week. Instead, put on the belt of truth to prepare and be ready for the enemy. Slip on the shoes of peace; so, when trouble lies ahead, we can be peace in the storm. Take hold of the shield of faith to block the arrows of evil. Equip yourself with the helmet of salvation, so when times are tough (like Monday morning), you have something to hold on too, and finally the sword of the Spirit. Use this weapon, so no matter what the situation is, you will be prepared to withstand. You can face the beginning of each week with courage and can light up the path you travel.

Self-Discipline

We all have dreams. But in order to make them become reality, it takes an awful lot of determination, dedication, discipline an effort. -Jesse Owens.

If your teen works or goes to school, they understand that Monday morning is not the most exciting day. It is all about the heart! Work as you're working for the Lord. That means make your work joyful, not a heavy burden. We often take life for granted; we are all guilty of this, as I have been. We are mad that we must get up and go somewhere to learn; so that one day, we can get the job that we love and provide for a family. I am homeschooled, so I have my own routine. I wake up at 7:00 am and start my schoolwork. If I get up and do that, I can get done with school around 2:00 pm. I try to get up every day and make my work as fun as possible. If your teen does not like mowing the lawn, then have them change it up. Have them listen to music or an encouraging message while working. Treat Monday as Friday, and work with a grateful heart. Self-discipline is to do everything excellent. My dad always tells us to be excellent in everything we do. He really emphasizes doing the little things well.

Practical Applications

Three ways you can help make Monday better;

1. Instead of complaining every Monday morning, thank God and pray that you can be the best you can be.

2. Encourage others around you, so they can encourage you. Spread positive energy to others that will put you and your coworkers in a good mood. Do not be an energy vampire!

3. Set goals, so that when Monday comes around, you can see how blessed you are to have a job that impacts others' lives.

Zach will introduce a most important skill your teen needs now, so they will be most productive to their family and community. This skill is known as a good work ethic.

TEENWORK: HOW TO INSPIRE YOUR TEEN TO LOVE WORKING

Once upon a time, a little over a century ago, there was a young boy named Walter. Walter was a dreamer. He loved to imagine and create ideas. Nothing could break his imagination down, even being physically abused by his father. His imagination was never lacking. As a young boy, he worked what jobs he could. At an early age his family moved to a farm where Walter developed a love for animals.

In 1911, his family moved to Kansas City, where he developed a love for trains. Young Walter worked a summer job for his uncle, a train engineer, selling snacks, and newspapers to travelers. He also developed a love for drawing and took art lessons at around the same time.

Then, he developed a love for serving his country. At age 16, Walter dropped out of school and applied for the army. But on account of his young age, he was denied the opportunity. Unfazed, he joined the Red Cross and drove an ambulance in France for a year.

Next, he revisited his love for drawing. After working for yet another newspaper, he decided to start his own animation business. By 1923, unfortunately, Walter had to declare his studio bankrupt, but Walter wasn't done. He created yet another studio with his brother, out in

California, but the studio began to fail. Walter was desperate for inspiration. On one of his train rides, Walter got bored. He sketched a character in his notebook he named Mortimer. He felt a strange connection to Mortimer, but his wife didn't approve of the name. So, Walter changed the character's name to Mickey. Mickey Mouse (Encyclopedia of World Biography) (www.notablebiographies.com).

Does that name sound familiar?

You know the rest of the story. Walt Disney went on to create one of the largest, most successful companies in the world, and set the standard for filming and entertainment with Disney Studios, but it didn't just start with a mouse. It started with a work ethic, and a drive to do whatever necessary to follow one's dreams.

Your teen probably doesn't face the struggles that Walter had to face. Your teen probably will never have the same trouble attaining a job or an education. Your child probably won't need a job at twelve years old like Walter did. But frankly, that's more of a problem than it is a benefit.

In the 21st century, most of us don't have to work 14-hour days to make our own food. Most of us don't have a grueling side job that takes up time too. We don't have to ride out to the fields, plant, harvest and reap to ensure we survive the winter. Mostly, that's a good thing, but there was a benefit in that lifestyle: It taught the importance of hard work, and no quitting allowed. Most Americans today have lost that. Here's an amazing statistic: According to a Gallup poll, up to 53% of Americans are disengaged from their job.

Gallup defines engaged as those "that are involved in, or enthusiastic about their job." That means over half the working class are not excited or enthusiastic in their current job. They have lost the work ethic and drive that dreamers and difference-makers possess.

Do you want your teen to become one of the 53%? Do want them to become an average Joe or Jane, or a Disney? A Spielberg? A Bill Gates?

Do you want them to become extraordinary? An Uncommon Teen? Of course you do!

Chances are your teen won't be as successful as Disney or a Spielberg or a Gates. However, your teen can become successful at whatever God gives them to do with a thriving work ethic, a strong foundation of self-discipline, and discipline from you, the parent.

Of course, success is a relative term, so I won't bother defining it, or predicting exactly *how* successful they will be. But, I can guarantee this: If your teen builds a healthy work ethic, and learns to enjoy and embrace the privilege of a job, they will make a difference and advance the kingdom of God in many ways. They won't just achieve worldly success; they will also achieve kingdom success.

If your kid doesn't know Proverbs 6:6-7, I highly recommend you read it to them. In fact, if you don't know it, start memorizing it right now. It says, "Go to the ant, thou sluggard; consider it's ways and be wise! It has no commander, no overseer or ruler, yet it stores its provisions in summer and gathers its food at harvest."

Now *that* is a challenging verse, one of your classic refrigerator types. It's applicable in almost every area of our life: our work, education, personal life, spiritual life, any area that requires discipline and perseverance.

Ants never seem to rest. Whenever they're not gathering or carrying food, they're trying to avoid our elephant feet and rebuild anthills we've damaged. Sometimes, I even feel sorry for them (Okay, *feel sorry* may be a little strong. I *sympathize* for them). They face so much danger and failure. But no matter what's going on, they work as hard as possible. Sure, they can lift things five hundred times their own weight, but what difference does it make? Do they use that strength to show off to the ladies and win prizes? No, they use that constantly every day working to provide food and shelter for themselves. We can all learn from examples like the ant.

The past couple paragraphs may seem like a cliché. This isn't just a cliché, it's the true word of God. If your teen gets that verse embedded in their brain, it'll help them out later in life. It's one of the many things you can do to strengthen their appreciation for working.

Volunteering and the Servant-Heart

Having a servant-heart is one of the greatest attributes your teen can possess. Volunteering can help strengthen that attribute and help it flourish into something beautiful and beneficial. Volunteering not only improves work ethic, but it also shows the importance and benefits of work. It teaches you to work harder *and* to appreciate and embrace hard work.

I'm not saying that your teen must become a life-long volunteer, and at every single opportunity sign them up. But face it, your teen probably hasn't volunteered for much yet. If they have, excellent. If not, talk to them about it. Look for opportunities for them to serve. Don't present it as an obligation, but as a privilege.

Experience has taught me that it is enjoyable to volunteer! Now, maybe that's just because I have a natural gift of being a servant, but it's true. Cayden, Jackson, and I volunteered with our homeschool group to help out with Operation Christmas Child in Dallas. It consisted of four to five hours of packaging, inspecting, and processing shoeboxes, and it was awesome. The people working there were so nice, and each time we filled a 40-pound shipping box full of Christmas shoeboxes, the satisfaction and joy of accomplishing our work was well worth the effort.

A youth group outreach in Dallas I was a part of reaped similar rewards. We were based in a poor neighborhood where several years earlier the people we worked with had built a community park. They hosted a block party for the kids, and we helped them make it possible. Also, their church desperately needed remodeling and reorganization. Of course, one does not just sit out and refuse to work on a church mission trip, so one might not call it volunteer work. But, it taught the youth the same thing: Working hard with all your heart and working for the Lord is satisfying, rewarding, and exciting. It sometimes depends on where your teen is volunteering, but everywhere that I've volunteered, it's been pretty much the same experience.

Cultivating a servant's heart in your child is one of the most important things you will ever do as a parent. If you teach them when they are young, if the seed is planted in their formative years and is allowed to flourish, it will grow into something amazing and bountiful in adulthood.

Also, you don't send your teen a couple hours away to some big event or corporation and have them help out for six plus hours. Even volunteering at a local church for an hour can be rewarding and reap the same results as working a full day somewhere else. Whether it's a church summer camp, a Vacation Bible School, community event or project, all of those are beneficial and will gradually instill a servant's heart in your teen.

I Came, I Saw, I Mowed

If your teen does not have some way of growing their work ethic, or no way of making some big bucks, I would encourage you to help them find one. I don't care how lazy or anti-work your teen is; pretty soon, they have to start earning some money (see Money chapter). In reality, it isn't that hard.

My first gig working a job was starting a little odd jobs company. My dad and I created it, even printing our own business cards with the name on it, Odd Jobs Unlimited. To give you some context, I really had no idea how to mow a lawn, or how to do any of the little yard work, around-the-house jobs that I was advertising. At least, so I thought.

My first job was mowing a guy's front and back lawn. I used his push mower, which was something I had never done before. To give you an idea of how challenging, stressful, and hard it was, my dad taught me how to use it in under five minutes. A lot of work, right? And I had never used a mower in my life! It was that easy.

I took over from there. The job took me between 1-2 hours to complete, and from what I remember, I did a good job for my first time. I went back to his house one more time, and then he sold it, not requiring my services any more. But, he paid me $20-$25 for mowing his lawn—almost twelve bucks an hour!

Those two mowing jobs were really the only two Odd Jobs Unlimited ever worked on. Shortly afterwards, I got the job that I've been currently working for over three years. But that was a great first job for me, and it is the same for practically every other teen. Here's why:

- It requires almost no skill.

- It is relatively easy, not strenuous

- The best part: You get seriously overpaid!

Unless you live out in the middle of nowhere (the boonies, as my northern relatives would say), odds are that there's a neighborhood within 15 minutes of your house with houses that own lawns, and those lawns need mowing. Who will mow the lawns? Up until this point, it has been the owner. But now, that's about to change.

Create flyers. Even go above and beyond like my dad—*my dad and I*—did, and order business cards. Start imagining the business your son can run for mowing lawns. It doesn't even have to be thought of as a business. It could just be a side hustle. Try to find customers that will bring your teen back to mow again. If they don't like the idea, show them how much it will benefit them in their future. Two hours per lawn for twenty bucks is *well* worth it!

What About Other Jobs?

It doesn't have to stop at mowing lawns. Weeding, weed whacking, yardwork, raking, sweeping, cleaning, etc. are all jobs your teens can perform. I once raked leaves for a guy. You would not believe how many leaves were lying on his roughly one-acre yard! That job took me well over ten hours to complete, on several different days working. If any job singly taught me the importance of working hard and unto the Lord, that one did. The first day, I took too many breaks. I didn't work hard enough. By the time I was finished, my work ethic blossomed and grew tremendously. Tutoring and babysitting can also be go-to jobs for your child. Also, one of the best ways for anyone to make money is to sell items they make themselves online.

Up until this point, I've addressed the guys. What about the girls? Mowing probably isn't their cup of tea. But weeding, raking, and gardening are all chores my mom does around the yard. Your daughter could do the same.

They can start babysitting. You can start by reaching out to friends who have younger kids or toddlers and ask them if they need a babysitter. Like mowing, babysitting doesn't require much skill, just a tenderness with children, a willingness to play and have fun, and a stern enough personality to reign rambunctious children back into line. Your daughter could also take up baking, dog walking, cleaning, etc.

Whatever the job may be, it can't just be all about making money. It's about working as unto the Lord, not for men (Colossians 3:23). It's about giving it your all, no days off. It's about developing the work ethic to use later in life when your teen will deal with a supervisor or when they have to work eight hours each day. They need to find joy in working. Proverbs 12:24 says, "The diligent find freedom in their work; the lazy are oppressed by work." (The Message). These are the keys to great teenwork. Teenwork develops into hard work, and hard work develops into joyful work.

In the next chapter, Cayden will discuss one of the biggest obstacles to hard work: electronics.

Your Child's Obsession with Electronics

Growing up in the twenty first century, most teens have social media, like Facebook, Instagram and SnapChat, just to name a few. While it can corrupt our world, it can also bring us together. Teen's these days are carrying access to the world in their pocket through a cellphone. One of the ways technology is being used is to express one's opinions. Some of these expressions can be useful, but the majority are harming your teen. People who use social media could be swaying your child's belief. Limiting your teen's "screen time," so to speak, is something you can do to help your teen's obsession. My family does an hour a day of electronics for about three to four days a week. Parents need to decide what boundaries they want for their family.

The World in Your Back Pocket

I knew a kid my age that seemed like a good kid, and acted like a good kid on the outside, but on the inside, he was not healthy. He went to church and did a Bible study with us, and you could say that he was a Christian. We were driving; and as I was sitting by him, I looked over, and he was searching something I would never repeat. "For nothing is hidden that will not be made manifest, nor is anything secret that will not be known and come to light" (Luke 8:17). The influence of technology is taking over the thoughts of our generation, and you must use your authority to stop it. With that said, technology has become the biggest distraction of our generation, and is causing many teens to be hypocritical in their actions and beliefs. Satan is using technology as a means to lead vast amounts teens into depression and anxiety through the constant pressures of social media. Our flesh wants to type or click inappropriate things because of our sinful nature. We are all sinners and need to overcome the flesh and temptation to not let technology control our thoughts and actions. It will take you, the parent/guardians, to stay in our business as technology will be a part of our world. Galatians 6:8 says, "Whoever sows to please their flesh, from the flesh will reap corruption; whoever sows to please the Spirit, from the Spirit will reap eternal life." Many teens, who are carrying the world in their pocket, have not taken into consideration this truth from the Scriptures.

W.H.O [World Health Organization] Announced "gaming disorder," Is That Your Teen?

Parents, I am not talking about Frogger, as you may have to explain this game to your teenager. I am talking about all these new games that teens are probably obsessed with. Now, there is a small percentage of families that do not allow video games. Here are some effects that today's games have on your teen. First, have you noticed any sudden charges on your credit card? The average player on some of these games are paying extra to enhance their playing ability. Second, mood changes are a major sign of obsession. For instance, being called for dinner with no response, being told to get off repeatedly, or telling them they can't play, which leads to arguments. Third, having horrible headaches, vision problems, and becoming sedentary are some of the symptoms from too much screen activity. Lastly, who is talking to your kid on these games? I know a kid who is 11 years old and plays video games nonstop; he has approximately 30 or 40 friends on these games and talks to all of them through the game. He knows very few of them. He told me he was talking to a grown man, and the guy was asking where he lived, how old he was, and what his name was. Thankfully, he did not say anything because he thought the guy was joking. It is important you are checking what games your teen is playing and who they are talking to. Remember, predators are some of the most patient people on the earth. No wonder World Health Organization has come up with a gaming disorder.
(https://www.who.int/features/qa/gaming-disorder/en/)

Teens Having Their Own Phone at A Young Age.

Majority of the teens I know, regardless of age, have their own phone. They are by themselves, and at times act secretive, seclude themselves, and seem to grow more insecure. Some of the parents are not doing anything about making sure these problems are not developing in your teen. With teens owning their own phone or device, the obsession is increasing because they have them at school, on the bus, in their room, and at their friend's house. For me, I cannot really relate to this because I do not have my own phone. To be honest, I do desire to have my own phone because the access it gives to information, and I enjoy the games they offer, but my parents do not think it is time. Also, I know many kids who are in the public school, and who are home schooled that have their own phone, so these devices are owned by all family dynamics. It is very difficult to find teens that do not own a phone. I know many teens that are insecure, secluded, and lack good social skills that a high level of screen time is causing. There are desires, like lust, which I think ranks at the top, that are being awakened at too young of an age because of the pull to explore the social media world. Some teens that I know, who have their own phone, have changed as a result of getting influenced by the technology world. Many of the negative influences were started by friends that exposed them to this new world. Have you ever thought about the world's most popular electronic symbol? A bitten piece of fruit! Hmm...

With Their Phone They Will Have the Urge to Text and Drive

I just finished a debate, through my co-op class, on texting and driving in Texas. I did a ton of research on the seriousness of texting and driving and was given the task to convince the judge and jury to repeal the law of texting and driving, especially during our teenage years. I was on the affirmative side and came to the debate with a ton of statistics for repealing this law. To name a few, 11 teens die each day because of texting and driving, 37,000+ people die each year because of automobile crashes in the U.S, and one out of four car accidents are caused by texting and driving. As a result of these statics, the textalyzer is a device that recently has been developed to detect if an accident was caused by texting. Do you have a teen that drives? If so, how are you monitoring texting and driving? This is really a self-control issue and maturity as we get older.

Having the Maturity to Own A Phone

Does your teen constantly beg for a phone? This more than likely means they probably are not mature enough to have it. Like I said, I know a ton of teens that have their own phone, and the teens that don't have one are jealous and begging their parents for one. Once the teens beg to get a phone, their parents get tired of the begging and end up giving in; and within a month, the teen either lost it or parents/guardian have found inappropriate material on it that brings stress and tension into the home. The desire to have a phone is now more common in pre-teens. Make sure your teen is mature enough to handle the smartphone; because if most adults cannot handle it, how will we be able to handle it? It seems that people are prisoners of their phones, maybe that is why it is called a "cell" phone. A suggestion to help hold off on a smartphone is get them a flip phone that can only call and text. The majority of teens do not need a smartphone because of their lack of maturity, lack of responsibility, and lack of self-control. Three questions to think about as you decide how to handle electronics with your teen: Is your kid mature enough to have a phone?, what social media restrictions will you need?, and if they drive, how will you enforce no texting? "As Jesus said in the Word of God, "with man this is impossible, but with God all things are possible" (Mathew 19:26). Electronics can become an addiction; and without God, it can almost be impossible to stop; so, if you have not given your life to Him, and are willing, you will see a drastic change in your parenting and your teens choices. Here is a great thought by Tony Reinke "smartphones do not invent new sins; they simply amplify every extant temptation of life" (Reinke). As Reinke says in *Twelve Tips to Parenting in the Digital Age*, "Once you give them a smartphone with a data plan, you move from having strong parental control to virtually none." In conclusion, even though I said before, I have a strong draw to electronics, but I know that at fifteen, I am not quite ready for full access to this world, and I am thankful for parents to help guide me through this stage of life. Here is an example of something you can do with your teen:

Age 13- flip phone

Age 16- smartphone

Age 18- social media

And this depends on your child's maturity.

CELL PHONE CONTRACT

1. I understand that the rules below are for my safety, and that my parents love me more than anything in the world. I understand that my parents want to give me freedom, while also giving me enough security to make smart choices. **Initial here**: _____

2. I promise that my parents will always know my phone passwords. I understand that my parents have a right to look at my phone whenever there's a need for them to do so, even without my permission. **Initial here**: _____

3. I will hand the phone to one of my parents promptly at _____ pm every school night and every weekend night at _____ pm. I will get it back at _____ am. **Initial here**: _____

4. I will not send or receive naked photos. Ever! I understand that there could be serious legal consequences that could put my parents and my future at-risk. **Initial here**: _____

5. I will never search for porn or anything else that I wouldn't want my grandma finding. **Initial here**: _____

6. I understand that my behavior on my phone can impact my future reputation—even in ways that I am not able to predict or see. **Initial here**: _____

7. I promise I will tell my parents when I receive suspicious or alarming phone calls or text messages from people I don't know. I will also tell my parents if I am being harassed by someone via my cell phone. **Initial here**: _____

8. When I am old enough, I won't text and drive. I understand it's very dangerous and pretty stupid. **Initial here**: _____

9. I will try to learn phone and internet etiquette. I understand this is an extension of normal manners. I will turn off, silence, and put my phone away in public–especially in a restaurant, at the movies, or

while speaking with another human being. I am not a rude person. I will not allow the phone to change this important part of who I am. **Initial here**: _____

10.   I will NEVER use my phone or social media to bully or tease anyone, even if my friends think it's funny. **Initial here**: _____

11.   I will not lie about where I have been or how I am using the phone. I promise to answer questions openly, honestly, and directly. **Initial here**: _____

I understand that this is NOT my phone, and that it was paid for by my parents. Having this phone is not a right; \it is a privilege that can be taken away. As such, I have read the following document and agree to the above rules. I understand that if I have any questions, I should talk to my parents face-to-face.

_____

Sign here

Now, in this chapter Zach will talk on one of the worlds' biggest struggles: money and its impact on this generation.

Money

Money. It's one of the things we literally *can't* live without. Maybe that's a bit of an overstatement, but seriously, if you don't have any money at all, you're in deep trouble. As a parent, you know firsthand how important money is and how key it is to manage and control it.

But not having enough money isn't the only potential problem when it comes to your finances; having too much can be even more deadly. The most well-known Bible verse when it comes to money is I Timothy 6:10, "The love of money is the root of all evil." Another key financial Scripture is Matthew 6:24, "You can't worship two Gods at once…you can't love both God and money." I Timothy 6:17-19 states, "Tell those rich in this world's wealth to quit being so full of themselves and so obsessed with money, which is here today and gone tomorrow. Tell them to go after God, who piles on all the riches we could ever manage—to do good, to be rich in helping others, to be extravagantly generous. If they do that, they'll build a treasury that will last, gaining life that is truly life."

Money is a huge Biblical topic. Jesus knew money was important. Throughout the Gospels, Jesus spoke more about money than any other subject. Tithing, taxing, giving, investing, it's all right there written in God's word!

Then why do so many of us, who know what Jesus says, who know what we should do, still make poor decisions when it comes to our money?

Maybe, it was because of parents. They didn't learn good money tips, so you had to figure them out for yourself.

Maybe, it's just plain laziness. Maybe you think it is too hard to manage your money. Maybe whatever method you've used is working, and you don't see a reason to change it.

Many Americans today live paycheck to paycheck. They're never able to visit distant family, whether in an emergency or for a reunion. They're not able to travel, or even to move out of their two-bedroom apartment into a comfortable house. Yes, part of it is the size of the salary; some don't make as much as they should. However, if you don't know how to wisely manage your finances, salary won't matter. Millionaires, even billionaires, higher financial advisors to help them spend their money wisely. Even *they* are afraid of losing all their money with one bad investment or decision. Why wouldn't the 99% of us who aren't super-rich fall into the same traps?

If you're reading this, and you're getting excited, thinking you'll learn a *ton* of fabulous tips on how to manage money, and thinking I'll throw a bunch of Dave Ramsey tips at you, then let me dash your hopes for a second. I'm not here to do that. I can't help you with your personal finances. I'm not your financial advisor, but I *can* make sure that you can pass along profitable tips and habits regarding money to your teen. I've made some questionable financial decisions in my life (granted, none much bigger than an impulsively bought $9 Dippin' Dots cup at the mall); and I know that if I continue to let those happen, I'll be headed towards mounds and mounds of student loan, credit card, and who-knows-what-else debt. But thankfully, I have a wise father, who leads me by example, and has taught me and my whole family beneficial habits when it comes to our finances. I'm here to pass some of those along, and a couple of my personal experiences, to you. Hopefully, you can pass them to your teen. Here we go.

Giving and Tithing

Before your child learns about investing and preparing for the future, they need to know the importance of giving and tithing. No matter what your financial situation is, you should always give. Proverbs 19:17 says, "If you help the poor, you are lending to the Lord—and he will repay you!" God is always faithful, so why wouldn't we be faithful with our money? Everything good thing comes from God, including money, so why wouldn't we give a little bit of our money back to God?

There is a story in the New Testament that illustrates that principle beautifully, in Mark 12: 41-44. "Jesus sat down near the collection box in the Temple and watched as the crowds dropped in their money. Many rich people put in large amounts. Then a poor widow came and dropped in two small coins. Jesus called to his disciples to him and said, "I tell you the truth, this poor widow has given more than all the others who are making contributions. For they gave a tiny part of their surplus, but she, poor as she is, has given everything she had to own."

Does this mean that God calls everyone to give away everything they have? Of course not! When Jesus confronted the rich man and told him to sell everything to the poor, it was because in order for the man to follow Jesus, he needed to destroy the number one idol in his life. Not all of us are so consumed with money and are greedy, but the story of the widow proves a point. It doesn't matter how much money you have; it is best to give all the time.

In II Corinthians 9 it says, "You must decide in your heart how much to give. And don't give reluctantly or in response to pressure. 'For God loves a person who gives cheerfully.'" That's the most

important part of giving. Don't do it so that you look good, don't do it reluctantly, don't even do it if you are just listening to the pressure of others. Now if God is pressuring you to give, you better listen.

If you haven't taught your child the importance of giving and generosity, do that before you ever talk to them about money in any other way, shape, or form. Teach them about tithing. Tithing is a blessing, but ultimately, you and your teen need to give as God is leading you. If it's more than 10%, trust God and do it. He knows what is best.

Your Teen Doesn't Need to Be Dave Ramsey

Now that we've talked about giving, it's time to focus a little more on the practical needs of money. How much allowance should you give (if any)? When should you start an investment plan? Maybe you have already helped your teen with these questions, and maybe you haven't.

First, let us talk about suggested tips for what your teens do with the money they earn. I work a part-time joy; plus, I get a monthly allowance for doing chores. Here's where all that money goes, percentage-wise:

Allowance money: $5 per week, $20-$25 per month

- 10%—tithe (always comes first)

- 10%-15%—savings (Suggested, I don't always take that much to put in)

- 75%-80%—I can do whatever I want with it: spending, offering, etc.

So, here's what happens at the end of all this: $2-$2.50 goes to tithe, $2-$3 goes to savings, and the remaining $15-$20 I can spend it and use it how I want. Sometimes a portion of that $15-$20 goes to savings, sometimes as offering (extra giving money), and sometimes I just keep it for spending money.

Let me tell you about my job. I work for a handyman; so, once I week, I work from around 8a.m. to 4p.m. assisting and helping him out whenever he asks me too. Not only am I learning some valuable life skills, but I've acquired several raises over the two to three years I've worked for him, and I've made several thousand dollars total. For each check I receive, here's where that money goes:

$60-$80 one day per week:

- 10%—tithe

- 45%—Roth IRA, or as we call it, a million-dollar fund

- 45%—Savings account

My dad and I are creating this plan, so I will have enough money to buy a car (in cash), eventually buy a house, etc. That money is what my savings account is. My parents put in a little bit when I was young; and now, I put money into it when I receive my check.

The retirement fund is pretty self-explanatory. I call it my millionaire dollar account. This money is the kind that gets invested into mutual funds. I receive interest on this money (Technically, I do get interest on my savings account, but that gets put in the bank. The interest in the Roth IRA, however, can increase, to an extent, exponentially).

But of course, you probably know what all of this stuff does anyway. You're an adult—you had to pay for college, buy a house, and a car, and you sure better have a retirement plan. You may have even saved and planned like I am when you were younger.

The question is, do you have a financial plan for your son or daughter? Are they going to be able to go to college without wallowing in thousands of student loan dollars when they're twenty or thirty? Will they have enough money for retirement?

The good news is, your teen doesn't need to know all of the top tricks and financial advice out there. He doesn't need to know how to invest in the stock market, but he or she should know what the stock market is. Your teen doesn't need to know exactly step-by-step how to apply for a student loan (Pray they never need one), but your teen needs to know what student loans are (so that they know how lucrative and evil they are). And luckily, it's pretty easy to start a basic plan with your teen to help them with their money.

You can't ask your kid to do this all on your own. Yes, some figure it all out by themselves (like my dad), but that might be when they're midway through college, already feeling the effects of student loans. And besides, these suggestions and tips are for your teens. You need to instill these principles in them during the few years they spend under your roof, RIGHT NOW! Otherwise, your teen will have to deal with all kinds of trouble.

If you have a plan for your kids already, you may still benefit from the suggestions I'm about to present. If you don't, I strongly suggest starting one as soon as you get done reading this chapter. You have no idea how much this will help both you and your teen to prepare for the future.

Some Tips and Tricks

You do need to instill some financial principles immediately. You've probably already told your child about tithing and giving, and maybe even some investing. That's great. By now they should also know what *unwise* money management is.

I'm not here to tell you that every soda and candy bar your teen buys will ruin him or her in the future, but if you haven't taught them about impulsive buying yet, tell them. When you see something that looks cool, sounds cool, tastes cool, whatever, resist the immediate impulse to buy it. If your teen sees something that they are interested in buying, and you feel kind of iffy about it, tell them to wait a couple of days. Resist the impulse.

What I really want to discuss, however, is for the long-term. What about college? First house? Retirement? What is your teen going to do?

Here's my college plan:

My parents have put in a certain amount of money each year into my college fund. It's a fair amount, but not nearly enough to pay for four years at a $25-$30,000 University. Luckily, I have the luxury of going to a junior college for two years, and those two years are both free. Your kids probably won't have that luxury, so I won't cover that. I still need more money though, so how am I going to earn it? The answer: scholarships.

Scholarships are super, super nifty, and will get your kids a long way, but they can be difficult to attain. So, my parents have invested a *ton* into my education. I took the PSAT as a sophomore. I hope to take several SAT's. I purchased a SAT training course. Those things will (hopefully and probably) get me enough money to where I take out minimal student loans. Here is a website that will show lots of ways to apply to get college scholarships https://clark.com/education/bestwebsites-resources-to-find-college/

As for a savings account, it's so easy to set one up, I'm not going to tell you how. I'll just tell you that my family uses Altra Credit Union (altra.org) to manage our savings accounts. You want to maximize your kids savings interest rate. If you keep your kids' savings rate at your local bank, you will receive less than 1% interest. I receive 5% interest at Altra until I'm 18. There are plenty of other online banks you can use for your kids savings account. This site will show you all of the top saving rates currently available www.bankrate.com

Roth IRA is an individual retirement account allowing a person to set aside after-tax income up to a specified amount each year. Both earnings on the account and withdrawals after age $59\frac{1}{2}$ are tax-free. When I was 13, my dad set me up a million-dollar fund. He told me that if I started putting 50% of the money I received during my teenage years and then 10-15% after I graduated from college, I would have over a million dollars when I was 60. I started putting 50% of the money I made into a Roth IRA; so, when I am 60, I can withdraw money from it tax free. There are many places you can start one. We started one at www.schwab.com, but there are other places you can do it also. If you want to use Schwab and start your kids million-dollar fund, here are the steps:

1. Go to www.schwab.com

2. Call Schwab at 866.855.9102

3. Tell them you want to start a Roth IRA for your kid.

4. They will tell you what application and forms to fill out

5. After you fill out all the forms, you will set the account online.

6. You will have to decide what mutual fund or funds to put his money into.

7. I have my million-dollar fund in their Schwab US Dividend Equity ETF. The ticker symbol is SCHD. You will need to do your own research and decide what to invest in. This is exciting for your kid and will give him some vision for his future. I started this over three years ago and now have over $4,000 in it, and I'm well on my way to a million dollars.

Remember that the poor plan for Saturday night, but the rich plan for the two or three generations. Help your kids plan for the future, so they just aren't planning for Saturday night.

In conclusion, let me say this: it is not the same for everyone. Some people start a college fund earlier, some later. Some start investing earlier, some later. Whatever you choose to do with your teen, pray about it first. History shows the earlier they start, the more their money will grow and the more opportunities you have to check the growth with them.

WORKS CITED

"Becoming an Adult: Why More Adolescents Now Say 'Don't Rush Me'."

The Christian Science Monitor, The Christian Science Monitor,

14 Jan. 2019, www.csmonitor.com/USA/Society/2019/0114/Becoming-an-adult-

Why-more-adolescents-now-say-Don't-rush-me.

Byers, Paula K., and Suzanne Michele. Bourgoin. "Walt Disney Bio." Encyclopedia Of World Biography, Gale, 2019.

Fiouzi, Andrew, and Mel. "In 2017, Is Marrying Your High School Sweetheart Still a Thing?" MEL Magazine, 5 Feb. 2019, melmagazine.com/.com/en-us/story/in-2017-is-marrying-your-highschool-sweetheart-still-a-thing.

Jaworska, Natalia, and Glenda MacQueen. " Adolescence as a Unique Developmental Period." Journal of Psychiatry & Neuroscience, Sept. 2015, jpn.ca/.

McClanahan , Harper C. "Father Absence and Incarceration ." Journal of Research on Adolescence, vol. 18, no. 1, 2004, doi:10.1111/jora.2008.18.issue-1.

Reinke, Tony. "Twelve Tips for Parenting in the Digital Age." Desiring God, 21 May 2018 www.desiringgod.org/articles/twelve-tips-forparenting-in-the-digital-age.

"THE FATHER ABSENCE CRISIS IN AMERICA." National Fatherhood

Initiative, Cdn2.hubspot.net.

"The Fatherless Generation." The Fatherless Generation,

23 Apr. 2010, thefatherlessgeneration.wordpress.com/.

Twenge, Jean. "The State of Students Today: An Interview with Dr. Jean

Twenge." Growing Leaders, 14 Feb. 2017, growing leaders.com/blog/state-students-today-interview-dr-jean-twenge/.

"12 Best Ways to Find College Scholarships." Clark Howard, 16 Oct 2019,clark.com/education/best-websites-resources-to-find-college/.

FAQ's

Chapter 1- Excellence

Q. How do I get my child a job?

A. If they are teens and you live in a neighborhood, your teen can knock on doors and ask if any work can be done at a fair wage. Think of people you know who remodel houses or have other manual labor jobs. These are great one or two day per week opportunities to learn skills and work ethic while earning a wage. Ask your teen their work interest and pursue an apprenticeship.

Q. How do I encourage excellence in my teen?

A. Set goals and talk to them about how excellent work affects their future in education, work, socially, spiritually, and physically. Take time during activities to work with your teen to use as teachable moments. The greatest teaching happens in the actual moment of success and adversity. As My father says," Good things, bad things, how are you going to react?"

Q. What if my child is insecure and is struggles interacting with people?

A. Model what you, as a parent, need to see in your teen. Show them how to be relational when opportunity arises. Teach them to introduce or reintroduce themselves each time they have opportunity. Talk about eye contact and firm handshakes. This helps builds confidence. Don't think you need to fix everything right now; it is in the heart of your teen. Catch them doing relational things and point them out (We all are at fault for pointing out flaws only).

Q. How do I get my child to speak in front of a crowd of people?

A. Encourage your teen to get up and speak. This build speaking skills, reduces stage fright, and increases security. Take advantage of opportunities to speak in front of small groups. Start with small presentations at home with family. Have them research a Bible figure and then present them as if they are a "live wax museum." Show them people who are great communicators. Teach them the benefits of speaking words of life and building people up. Teach them that words have weight, and negative words should carry no weight, but positive words carry weight and should receive the most attention.

Chapter 2- To Date or Not to Date

Q: My high school daughter is currently dating. It seems as though you wrote this chapter by primarily addressing the guys. Any advice for me and my daughter?

A: If she is willingly participating in the relationship, talk to her about it. Figure out what draws her to the guy, and determine if you believe him "worthy" enough of your daughter. Character is everything. If you question his character and his motives, be wary. Warn her of the potential consequences, and make sure you have her best interests at heart. Don't necessarily try to scare her out of it, but at least make sure she knows how big of a decision she is making. If she doesn't want to be a part of the relationship, then you might have to confront the guy about it if he still wants to pursue her.

Q: Whenever I confront my son/daughter about their boyfriend/girlfriend, they become defensive and say that I need to give them more freedom. What should I do?

A: At this stage in their life, you as the parent know what is best for them more than they do. Remind them of that, but don't come across as impatient and overbearing. Tell them you have their best interests at heart, and that you truly care about them. Before you confront their dating relationship, you first need to make sure that you retain your position as the ultimate and loving authority in their life. Once you have their trust, then it'll be easier to convince them to stop dating.

Q: I personally don't view dating as a negative thing, until it gets explicit and sexual. That's why I allow my kids to date in high school. What do you say to that?

A: I'm not going to tell you straight up that you are wrong, but getting in a dating relationship only raises the percentages of your teen becoming involved with somebody explicitly and sexually. If you trust your kids to stay pure, and you believe that you as the parent can keep your kids in check, then it is not the end of the world if you allow them to date. I've just written this chapter to make you aware of the temptations and the negatives of dating in high school. If you honestly believe that dating in high school won't hurt your kids, fine; if not, then do something about it. Don't just do enough so your kids don't cross the line; do enough to the point that they don't even come close to crossing it.

Q: I'm suspicious that my teen has been hiding a boyfriend/girlfriend from me and aren't telling me everything. What should I do?

A: If talking to them isn't working, then you might have to do some snooping. Since you have their best interests at heart, it's totally within your rights as a parent. Do a spontaneous phone-check. If you suspect they're skipping school or other activities, ask them questions. Eventually, if you suspect they are still hiding, ask them straight up. Ask with love and care for your teen. If you ask in a demanding and mean way, they will get scared and continue to lie.

If you had to snoop around a little, be prepared; your teen will probably accuse you of sneaking and being dishonest. But then again, so were they. You as the parent need to take control and establish yourself as their authority.

Chapter 3- Friends

Q. What are some ways you can nurture good friendships in your teenager?

A. Several qualities to teach your teen healthy friendships are: be honest, restore misunderstandings, show appreciation for loyalty, be compassionate instead of critical and do not base friendship off of your expectations only. No one can meet our expectations, so extend grace in your relationships.

Q. What is the "right" friend?

A. The right friend gives more than they take, lives with an "open hand" concept instead of "closed fist" where they are constantly in defense and fight mode, cares about what your teen sees, hears, and thinks, and is most concerned with your teens faith in Jesus Christ and walk with Him.

Q. Should my teen try and change a negative friend?

A. I have to answer this with the truth of God's word. If bad company ruins good morals, as theBible states, your teen needs to be careful thinking they can change them. They need to love them and tell them they can spend quality time when they begin striving to live a godly example. Living the Word of God in front of them is the best possible chance for change.

Chapter 4- Your Outgoing Teen

Q: I want to foster, but my life is just so busy. How can I help others foster?

A: If you know someone who fosters, make them a meal and pray for them. When you think life is hard, think of them. Show as much support to them as possible, or there is respite where you can let that person have a night out, and you get certified to take care of them.

Q: What do you mean when you say, "find others in need"? How do I do that?

A: When you try to help your teen, you are serving God. If you and your teen can't treat each other the way Jesus intended, then you can't treat the homeless and those less fortunate the right way. You can put a fake face on and act like everything is okay, but it's not from the right heart.

Q: My friend fosters. What are some ways I can help them?

A: Well, I am sure that they could always use a warm meal. My mom always says the best meal are the ones she doesn't have to make. Sign up for respite, which is taking care of the kids for a few hours. Always pray, no matter what. Give them encouraging Bible verses Etc. Send them daily reminders of why they do what they do.

Chapter 5- The Gift of Encouragement

Q. How can I encourage when I notice my teen slip into depression?

A. Develop calluses on your knees in prayer for your teen. Do not lose your child's heart. If you do, they will tune you out. Teens will listen to those they believe like them. Do not get irritated by them, but love them. When talking to your teen, listen for the cracks, and get to the core of the issue. Love them through their faults and failures. Q. How do I encourage my timid teen?

A. Help with fear of talking in front of people by getting your teen to step out of their comfort zone. Do not question him or her on why he or she is shy or quiet just offer encouragement. Here are six ways to get your teen to open up: get interested in their interests, create more family time, start the conversation wisely. Listen, no matter what. Be understanding, and lend them a hand. Q. How do I encourage my teen?

A. Encourage even the smallest effort. Stop finding fault with the wrong, and applaud the right. Look for outwardly demonstrable ways to encourage your teen. Reject negative responses, and make positive comments.

Chapter 6- How to Destroy the Root of All Sin

Q: How do I get my teen to confess?

A: You never make them, you just let them know you are there for them, and the punishment is the pain of sin. Don't punish for what they did, reward for what when they come to you for help. Then help them by holding them accountable. To prevent, you can give them bible verses or words of encouragement. The more you talk to them and stay open to them, they will naturally feel convicted and want to start talking.

Q: How do I "train" my teen to do the right thing?

A: Tell them what you require of them. What are your expectations? Also, you need to be an example to them. For example, you tell your teen not say bad words, but you do. You are your teens biggest role model, whether you like it or not. They see what you do therefore they will do the same. Set the example.

Q: My teen hates spending time with me he says I am boring, what do I do?

A: I think that it goes back to the quality time. Be intentional about slowing down and making time for them. Let them choose a book that you could read together. I am 13, and I love when my mom does a read aloud. It may sound childish, but if the book is of interest, then it will be good, which leads to more time together.

Q: When you say staying away from sin, how do I help them with that?

A. Watch for what makes them sad or mad, mood changes or friends that rub off their sinful ways on to your teen. Television can be a distraction, and phones can steal quality time because they seem to consume attention once they are picked up and many are exploring content that is damaging their soul. School can be good for your kid, yet it can be very bad too since bullying is a real problem. Many negative behaviors result from inappropriate talk at school and other social teen settings.

Q: I try to do everything I can to protect my child, but many days something happens that was bad.

A: School can be a great enemy for teens because so many of them are insecure and like to gossip and spread bad rumors. This is one of the reasons my parents chose the homeschool route. My family and I spend time reading the bible and discussing it during the school day, helping us stay drawn to the light of Christ. Many of my friends go to public school and seem to carry a lot of burdens they weren't meant to carry. Praying with your teen is the greatest way to send your teen when they leave your home and go into the world.

Chapter 7- Good Dad, Great Dad

Q: I'm a single mom. What do I do?

A: If you are part of a church or some other type of fellowship, I highly recommend finding some man to mentor your son. It could be someone you already know (which would be far easier), or someone you believe can develop a strong bond with your son. Personally, I've always had a strong relationship with my dad, but there are several other godly men in my life who I am very close with. You don't have to necessarily find someone to become a father for your son. You need to find someone who can become a mentor, a friend, a helper. Someone who cares.

Q: My job requires me to work longer days, and I'm not able to spend enough quality time with my kids. What should I do?

A: As I've already stated in the chapter, pray about it. Ask God if he wants you to quit and start afresh, or if you should just modify your schedule. And if you're ever on a long business trip away from your kids, find time out of your day to call them or Facetime them. The duration doesn't matter as long as the quality of the time you are spending with your teens. But still try to find enough time where quality time becomes readier and more available.

Q: My son and I have always been close, but of late our relationship has become a bit stale. How do I preserve our relationship?

A: There are many various reasons why this may be happening, so I'll just explain what you should do to revive the bond. If you haven't been seeking out quality time of late, start doing that again. Play games. Watch movies together. Take him out to a game, or for dinner. Ask him about some of the important things in his life (school, sports, girls, etc.). Of course, you should always be doing these, even when the father-son bond is thriving, but doing these activities together will help bring you closer together. If they don't work, then there's something much deeper and darker at work, so confront him about it and pray for him.

Q: I'm a father, and I have a daughter (or two, or three, etc.) You wrote this chapter seemingly just about the father/son relationship. What about the daddy/daughter relationship?

A: The daddy/daughter relationship is just as important as the father/son relationship. The principles in this book can be used in your daddy/daughter relationship.

Chapter 8- Walking from Death to Life

Q: My son/daughter does not like to pray or go to church; how can I spark his fire?

A: Well, you can't force them to pray, fall in love with Jesus, or have them read read their bible. It starts with you modeling all these characteristics as a follower of Jesus that you want them to have. Make sure you are reading and praying for and with your teen, take time before bed to read a chapter, and then discuss what it meant. Your goal is to have your teen own his or her own faith and not live off yours when they leave home.

Q: My teens don't pray out loud; they say it's too embarrassing. What do I do?

A: Do you pray out loud? If not, they see what you do, and they follow. Be a good example in everything. Just ask them who they are praying to; is it for the people who are listening, or the Lord? Help them get in a quiet place where distractions are minimized. Teach them to pray at the dinner table, with you before bed, and with extended family. This will increase confidence and boldness.

Q: How can I make praying a little less awkward?

A: Model more of it. My mom prays over everything, for the small things of trying to find something, to our safety and health. Don't be embarrassed; if their friends think of them as the "holy one," encourage that is what the goal is as a follower of Jesus.

Q: My teen always want to pray at the table, and I think it's great, but I don't think it is for the right reason. How can I change that?

A: Above all else, keep encouraging them to pray. Continue to mold your teen by modeling for your teen. Talk to them about why we pray, but do not discourage praying.

Chapter 9- T.G.I.M. Teen

Q: How can I have integrity when no one is around?

A: Find someone to hold you accountable and read God's word and see what he requires. Pray and find out how you can help others. Find out what draws you to sin and destroy it. Remove yourself when temptations come your way and stay in the light.

Q: Why would I believe in God's word if I don't understand all of it?

A: If everyone knew everything, then why would anyone need God? If you understood everything, you would have no need to seek Godly knowledge and wisdom because you know everything. Life wouldn't have meaning. Instead of trying to figure everything out, obey and live out the things you do know. The Word of God says to ask, seek and knock and the door will be open to you. We must remember, it is a living word and no one will ever know it all has to teach.

Q: My job is boring; how can I make Monday more exciting?

A: Think about your family and why you're working. If you don't have multiple members to care for, take pride in providing for yourself. A lot of people don't have jobs, so maybe your job is boring, but the fact that you have one is a blessing. Sixty-one percent of the world's people don't have a job opportunity, so consider yourself blessed.

Q: I want to pray, but I can't seem to find time.

A: Many times, we cannot give the Lord five minutes, but He gave His one and only son to die for us. He gives time for us, so we need to spend time with Him. Set aside time each day that is quiet and has limited distractions. It's like someone who gives you a gift, but you don't receive it. Prayer is a gift! It is communication with the one who created us! This is hard for me as well, but I will say, there is no better way to spend our time than in prayer.

Q: I can't seem to spend time with my teen; he always turns me down. How can I get him to talk or desire to spend time?

A: Well, try to find things that interest him, such as sports, music, etc. Family time does not have to be boring; Play board games, or do a read aloud. Create an atmosphere that helps you bond and eventually they will open up. (Hint: many of us teens like to talk later at night). These times will create a comfortable and safe place for them which will result in more time they will want to spend with you.

Chapter 10- Teenwork: How to Inspire Your Teen to Love Working

Q: How can my teen earn money and learn hard work without having an actual job?

A: Re-read the section on volunteering. That's the best way to teach a strong work ethic to anyone. But yes, I understand. Your teen needs to earn money as well. One way to do it is allowance. If you don't give out a monthly allowance to your teen for doing chores around the house, start doing that. They're working for you essentially; they deserve to get paid. I get paid 5$ a week for doing the weekly chores around the house, which adds up to $20-$25 a month. Start doing this with your teens, and create your own plan.

Q: I can't get my teen out of the house. He's too busy on his phone or with homework. What do I do to improve his work ethic?

A: The answer is right there in the question. Your teen doesn't have to leave the house. Homework is perhaps one of the most valuable ways your kids can discipline themselves to get the work done and not procrastinate. Just make sure your teen is working hard and diligently when it comes to their schooling. As for the phone, reread the electronics chapter. Make sure that they do not wallow in a spirit of laziness, but bask in a spirit of joyfulness and hard work

Q: Speaking of homework, my teen is not doing well at school, and I don't want them working too much now since school is our top priority.

A: You are absolutely right. If your teen is failing grades or just not doing well and you want them to succeed, go for it. You don't need to give them the extra burden of a job *and* school. Now if they are struggling with keeping good grades, make sure they are staying focused with school. If they are trying their best and simply failing, help them out. If you deem it necessary, get them a tutor. They obviously have the work ethic and determination to succeed. If they aren't staying focused, determine the cause. Working a part-time job can be very useful, but at this point in life, education is a top priority.

Chapter 11- Your Child's Obsession with Electronics Q.

How do I as a parent manage my teens device usage?

A. Make sure your phone is synced to your teen's phone, so you can monitor their social media usage. Have your teen turn his or her phone to you at an early time in the evening. Continually, check apps, photos, text messages, and emails to hold them accountable. Helpful hint: Click on each app to make sure they are not hiding anything underneath.

Q. How can I help protect what my teen sees?

A. Purchase software that filters content, blocks chats, monitors social media sites, and monitors all self-phone usage. Create ground rules that allow for open conversations. Keep all electronics in a central location in the house. My family has a software called Covenant Eyes that helps filter inappropriate content.

Q. How do I handle one-on-one device implementation in education systems?

A. Take time to read the electronic code of conduct with your teen. Go through the device like you would a personal device. Contact the education administration if you sense or find inappropriate use as they can retrieve content searched or viewed.

Q. How do I know my teen is ready for a smartphone?

A. Ask why your teen needs a smartphone. How responsible is your teen? Are you willing to write a contract with your teen, and what is the trust level of communication between you and your teen?

Chapter 12- Money

Q: How do I handle my teen's financial decisions? i.e., phone bills, car, auto insurance, etc.

A: For the phone, what my parents are doing is paying for the phone per month, but on 4G. No unlimited. Plus it's on a cheap network, only $9 a month. For the car and auto insurance, I'm going to pay for that. But I can't afford that right now, even if I could drive. That's why I'm going to buy a car around 18. By that age, I'll be able to pay for the car and the auto insurance and any other car fixups. I recommend you do the same with your teen.

As for other minor things like Spotify premium, XBOX Gold, and other minor payments, let your teen handle those. I personally don't mind too much the ads on Spotify, so I don't pay the extra 10$ for no ads and unlimited skips. If your teen really gets peeved by inconveniences such as these, let them pay to fix it. However, make sure that they don't spend *all* their money on things that aren't that necessary. My parents have numerously cautioned me against impulsive buying. I don't need to spend $20-$25 a month on things I don't need.

Q: I don't believe in allowance. How else can my teen earn money?

A: If you haven't found them a job yet, do that. Whether it be mowing, working part-time for someone or even hooking them up with a friend of yours who's willing to pay for labor, etc. It's money in the bank. Now if you can't do that, then an allowance is the simplest, easiest way for your teen to earn money. But don't lose hope; either reach out or have your teen reach out, and somebody will respond with an opportunity.

Q: My teen says he/she deserves a car. What should I do?

A: If they want you to pay for it, put your foot down and tell them to wait (unless you are rich and can easily afford a car and insurance.) Odds are your teen doesn't need a car right now anyway.

If your teen is willing to pay for it, make sure you are still a key part of making the decision. If they don't need a car, they shouldn't need one even if they can pay for it.

My dad's first car was a used, red Mazda GLC, but he was eyeing a purple Dodge Charger. His dad cautioned him against buying the Charger, since it was more expensive and cost more for maintenance and gas. He didn't tell my dad specifically what to do, but he gave wise advice, which my dad eventually listened to. Do the same for your child. If they want to buy a car, they are probably at the age when they can start making more decisions on their own. However, that doesn't mean you are excused from offering advice. Tell them what you would do. Make sure they don't regret their decision.

Made in the USA
Columbia, SC
17 March 2025